Christian—

We Miss

Paul H. Elliott

Al Gibson

EXEMPLARY PERFORMANCE

EXEMPLARY PERFORMANCE

Driving Business Results by Benchmarking Your Star Performers

Paul H. Elliott, PhD
Alfred C. Folsom, PhD

JOSSEY-BASS
A Wiley Imprint
www.josseybass.com

Jacket design by Jeff Puda
Elliott photo by Nathaniel P. Elliott
Folsom photo by Christopher & Rachel Lauen

Published by Jossey-Bass
A Wiley Imprint
One Montgomery Street, Suite 1200, San Francisco, CA 94104-4594—www.josseybass.com

Jossey-Bass books and products are available through most bookstores. To contact Jossey-Bass directly
call our Customer Care Department within the U.S. at 800-956-7739, outside the U.S. at 317-572-3986,
or fax 317-572-4002.

Wiley publishes in a variety of print and electronic formats and by print-on-demand. Some material
included with standard print versions of this book may not be included in e-books or in
print-on-demand. If this book refers to media such as a CD or DVD that is not included in the version
you purchased, you may download this material at **http://booksupport.wiley.com**. For more
information about Wiley products, visit **www.wiley.com**.

Library of Congress Cataloging-in-Publication Data
Elliott, Paul H.
  Exemplary performance : benchmarking star performers for business results / Paul H. Elliott,
Alfred C. Folsom.—1st ed.
    p. cm.
  Includes index.
  ISBN 978-1-118-20420-7 (cloth); ISBN 978-1-118-24076-2 (ebk.); ISBN 978-1-118-26557-4 (ebk.);
ISBN 978-1-118-22844-9 (ebk.)
  1. Employee motivation. 2. Employee selection. 3. Employees—Attitudes. I. Folsom, Alfred C., 1961-
II. Title.
  HF5549.5.M63E45 2013
  658.3′125—dc23

                                                                    2012034923

Printed in the United States of America
FIRST EDITION

HB Printing   10 9 8 7 6 5 4 3 2 1

This book is dedicated to my loving family, who have provided unfailing support for me throughout my career and particularly during the writing of this book:

Debbie, my wife, who has brought both grace and beauty into our relationship

Isaac (1979–2003), who never forgot that his name meant laughter and was a constant source of joy throughout his brief life here on earth

Luke, who has always been an inspiration for me when I encounter his consistent optimism in the midst of life's challenges—I appreciate his wisdom in bringing Jody into my life.

Nathaniel, whose creativity and drive have already impacted people around the world—I appreciate his wisdom in bringing Aletheia into my life.

Paul H. Elliott

Annapolis, Maryland
July 30, 2012

————

For my family, who richly bless me every day: Vanessa—my wife, partner, and best friend, who has always pointed me in the right direction and provided loving support and encouragement, particularly during the writing of this book. Julia, who inspires me daily with her gifts and service. And George—my constant source of enthusiasm and joy. I also dedicate this book to my mother, Drucilla Faulkner (1937–2012)—a tremendous encourager to me, always.

Geneva, Alabama
July 30, 2012

Appreciation

It is often challenging to attribute ideas and models precisely, because they evolve over the years. However, in our case, we have both been shaped significantly by the writing, tools, and mentoring of Dr. Joe Harless. His deep insight into the performance of people in work settings, combined with his expertise in developing tools to equip others to improve that performance, is without peer. This book and the models it represents are deeply dependent on his thoughtful career.

Mark Morrow provided significant editorial support to both of us throughout this project. Paul was additionally supported by Debbie Elliott, whose meticulous eye brought greater clarity to his writing. We also thank the rest of the team at Exemplary Performance, LLC, whose insights are embedded throughout.

Contents

Defining
the Opportunity

CHAPTER ONE

The Value of Leveraging the Insights of Your Stars

In This Chapter

- A Flawed Assumption
- The Real Value of Stars
- Shifting the Performance Curve
- Activity Versus Accomplishment
- The Value Proposition for This Book

As a leader, you begin every day with options on how to improve the performance of your organization. You can shift your strategy, enter new markets, invest in new products, or acquire a competitor. You can also jump on another bandwagon—talent management, Six Sigma, lean manufacturing, advances in cost accounting, off-shoring various business operations, and so forth. All of these alternatives are valid and can drive shareholder value. They also are costly to implement and consume significant management attention.

We want to provide you with an additional option—a model for driving improved business results by replicating the accomplishments of your star performers. The advantage of this approach is that it is derived from the current performance of those stars, so you know that it is possible within your current structure and culture. It also has the advantage of being cost-effective and quick.

This method is based on capturing the performance profile of your stars and then using this information to quickly enable significant improvement in the results produced by the remainder of your workforce. Along the way, we want to change your ingrained assumptions about the relationship between innate talent and high performance. *The correlation is not as significant as you probably assume.* Read on, because you'll be convinced that the great preponderance of your people can shift their performance to more closely replicate the results you so highly value in your top performers.

Let's start by providing a solid working definition of a term we use throughout the book—"stars." *Stars are those teams and individuals who consistently produce the greatest RESULTS in support of the organization's strategy and goals.* These performers may not have the most talent (or potential), but they translate the talent they do have into meaningful outcomes that drive business success.

A Flawed Assumption

When we encounter true talent—the musical prodigy, the athletic wunderkind, the business genius—we are awed. How do they do it? We think to ourselves, "If only I had been born with those gifts, I would be a star, too."

We all labor under the assumption that there is a defined and limited supply of talent (innate ability) and that only a few individuals have what it takes to become true stars in their professions. While this assumption may hold some validity for Olympic-level athletes and top-tier entertainers, the flaws of applying such a broad assumption to the workplace are easy to identify.

For example, most of us still buy into the assumption that our success (the organization's and our own) is wholly dependent on how many high-performing stars we are able to hire and retain. We search frantically for these extraordinary individuals (we even call this search the "war for talent") and then rely on this limited number of star performers to drive the success of the entire team.

An Alternative

We want you to step back from this assumption long enough to test our alternative. Let's test the assumption that an organization's *talent curve* does not predetermine its *performance curve*. In other words, our experience across multiple clients in disparate industries shows that it is possible to *replicate* the results of your stars without replicating their innate talent and ability.

Your organization's talent curve does not predetermine its performance curve.

Perhaps you're saying, "Time out! Are you telling me that I can succeed with people who are not talented?" No, that's not what we are saying at all! What we are saying is this: the exceptional results that are consistently produced by your exemplary performers are not dependent on talent alone. Talent explains some of the results turned in by these high-performing individuals, but it is not the whole story. We want to fill in the significant gaps in the old talent-centric narrative and empower readers to create a new narrative that leads to a much higher portion of the workforce producing exceptional results. We want to support you in producing more high performers within your current workforce.

In his 2008 book, *Talent Is Overrated: What Really Separates World-Class Performers from Everybody Else*, Geoff Colvin makes the following points based on his synthesis of years of research:

- Talent (innate ability) does *not* account for the variance in performance seen in music, athletics, or business.
- Intelligence and memory do *not* account for it either.
- The single largest contributor to exemplary performance is deliberate practice.[1]

"Deliberate practice is characterized by several elements, each worth examining," Colvin writes. "It is actively designed specifically to improve performance, often with a teacher's help; it can be repeated a lot; feedback on results is continuously available; it is highly demanding mentally."[2]

Colvin also cites a study by Anders Ericsson that includes the following statement: "The differences between expert performers and normal adults reflect a life-long period of deliberate effort to improve performance in a specific domain."[3]

The Real Value of Stars

If you take a moment and think about the individuals who work in your organization, you can likely call out a few stars who consistently produce exceptional results. They are easy to spot and are usually the ones who tackle each day, with its opportunities and challenges, by exhibiting consistent energy and engagement. In your role as a leader, you appreciate these exemplary performers because they not only make your job easier, but they also provide significant returns to your organization.

Bill Gates, the founder of Microsoft, once stated that if he had lost the top five performers in his company during its formative years, Microsoft would never have become the company it is today. In sales organizations, it is common for performers in the top 10% to generate 30% to 50% or more of the revenue. In software engineering, the top programmers often write ten times the amount of bug-free code as do average performers. How large is the gap between the results of your stars and the results of solid but average performers? If you measured it, the difference is likely astounding. What if you were able to move even a small percentage of these average performers to star status? The results for your company would be game changing!

It is important to realize that the dramatic differences described here are between best performers and good performers and not between best performers and poor performers.

Our research and practice indicates that for complex, knowledge-based work, the difference between moderate and star performers exceeds 50%. In other words, the highest-performing sales teams are producing 50% greater revenue than average-performing sales teams. This amazing ratio also means that the best-performing teams in R&D are bringing 50% more products to market, or doing it 50% faster (or both) than average teams. The ratio also means that the best maintenance technicians return the line to full production significantly faster than merely good technicians. It is important to realize that the dramatic differences described here are between best performers and good performers and *not* between best performers and poor performers.

Imagine the Possibilities

Imagine the possibilities in your organization if you acted on the premise that the talent curve does *not* predetermine the performance curve? What if you could create models of optimal performance based on the insights of your stars? (Chapter Four describes how to capture these models, which we call Profiles of Exemplary Performance.) You would be able to:

- Assign all of your employees to jobs that enabled them to perform at the top of their game with the right skills and tools for meeting and exceeding their goals and objectives.
- Provide clear expectations so that everyone in your organization knew exactly what was expected of them; there would be no conflicting goals and feedback would be timely and accurate.
- Create a work environment and culture that was conducive to outstanding performance on a day-in and day-out basis.
- Ensure that everyone in the company, from bottom to top, felt as if they were integral members of a successful team.

What would be the impact if you closed the gap between average performers and star performers by 10, 20, or 30%? At the most basic level, that's what this book is about: how you can achieve greater business results by enabling exemplary performance throughout your organization. Notice the verb "enabling." According to the *Merriam-Webster Dictionary* it means:

1. to provide with the means or opportunity
2. to make possible, practical, or easy[4]

When a new hire joins an organization, both employer and employee have nothing but optimism and hope for a grand and successful future together. Can you imagine how your organization would thrive if your teams and individuals were as successful as they intended to be on the day they were hired? Helping organizations move toward this highly productive state is the theme of our practice.

What happened to these new hires—bright-eyed, with a spring in their step and a smile that is contagious? What happened to their optimism, enthusiasm, infectious energy, and commitment? Whatever it was that chipped away at this "honeymoon" level of engagement is potent, because all too soon there is a pitched battle between organizational reality and the new hire's enthusiasm. Typically, within six months, organizational reality is the hands-down victor. The new hire often mutters bitterly, "How did I get myself into this mess?" What can we, as leaders, do to avoid this disillusionment and sustain the initial engagement?

"If you pit a good performer against a bad system, the system will win almost every time. We spend too much of our time 'fixing' people who are not broken, and not enough time fixing organization systems that are broken."

—Rummler and Brache, 1995

Perhaps Geary A. Rummler and Alan P. Brache characterized this classic battle best in *Improving Performance* (1995): "If you pit a good performer against a bad system," they wrote, "the system will win almost every time. We spend too much of our time 'fixing' people who are not broken, and not enough time fixing organization systems that are broken."[5]

"Hold on!" you might be thinking. "My company has great processes and systems and our workforce is committed and performance excellent." While you may be correct, our challenge is to at least take a serious look at the variance between your good, solid performers and your stars. We'd be willing to bet that a closer look would likely reveal some significant upside potential and that diagnosis would show some substantial holes in the entire spectrum of work systems that have a direct impact on your individual performers and teams. Our research and experience tell us that you need to align six distinct work systems in order to enable exemplary performance (see Figure 1.1). These systems are:

- Expectations and Feedback
- Rewards, Recognition, and Consequences
- Motivation and Preferences
- Skills and Knowledge
- Capacity and Job Fit
- Environments, Systems, and Resources

Figure 1.1. Exemplary Performance System Model

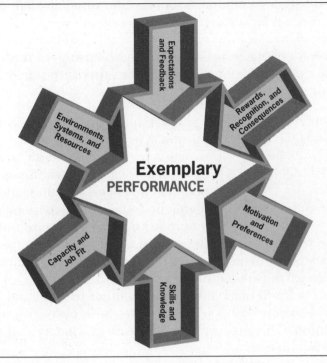

Source: Exemplary Performance, LLC. Copyright 2008–2012.

The primary accomplishment for high-performing leaders is creating a powerful team of high-performing direct reports.

If these six support systems are not mutually reinforcing, the scenario of your new hire's growing disengagement will be played out again and again. As a leader, your job is to be an architect who integrates and aligns work systems in a way that enables all of your team to more closely replicate your stars. Another way of stating this is that the primary accomplishment for high-performing leaders is creating a powerful team of high-performing direct reports.

As an architect of star performance, you must ask for and obtain honest answers to these vitally important questions:

- Are the outputs and expectations for my team—and those of the other teams in my department or division—aligned?

- Do individual team members have a clear understanding of their direct contribution to shareholder value through the work they perform and the results they produce?
- Are the right resources consistently available just in time?
- Do you—or your team—participate in activities or meetings that are perceived not to add value or support the attainment of your objectives?

Most organizations unintentionally create barriers that inhibit high performance.

These questions might seem basic, but you'd be surprised how many companies have not sufficiently answered them or implemented solutions to the potential problems that these questions highlight. In fact, our experience shows that most organizations have not taken the time to intentionally design the requisite systems to enable exemplary performance. Instead, most organizations unintentionally create barriers that inhibit high performance.

This book will help you tear down those barriers and enable individual performers to achieve greater business results for your organization. This process is at the heart of what we call *shifting the performance curve*.

Shifting the Performance Curve

Simply put, shifting the performance curve is all about driving results, enhancing revenue, and improving margins. Our

Shifting the performance curve is all about driving results, enhancing revenue, and improving margins.

model and methodology allow organizations, their leaders, and associated work teams to capture more value with existing resources. In a "do more with less" economy, this is the right strategy for these times, clearly differentiating you from your competition.

The underlying premise for replicating your stars is that exemplary performance is not reserved for just a few individuals. Exemplary performance is an achievable goal for the great majority of executives, managers, teams, and individual contributors. Take a look at Figure 1.2. It represents the distribution of employees within one function or role in a company (sales, R&D,

Figure 1.2. The Performance Curve

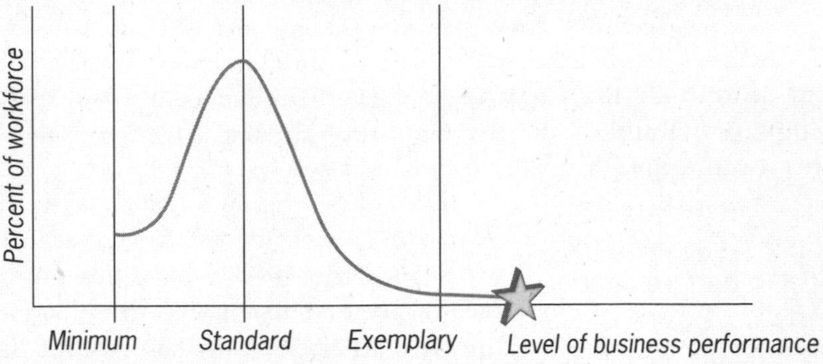

Source: Exemplary Performance, LLC.

customer service, and so on). The horizontal axis represents meaningful outputs (business results, accomplishments)—not talent, skills, competencies, or any other form of input.

The great bulk of your team is meeting expectations in the center of the distribution, as represented by the vertical line labeled "standard." However, we all recognize that some team members, day in and day out, produce exceptional results. These stars are represented by the star on the far right of the graph.

This star performer might be a skilled tradesperson who can restore a manufacturing line to full functionality in half the time of anyone else at the plant, or perhaps the star performer is the customer service rep who routinely translates irate customers into loyal fans.

You can surely think of many other examples from your own work experience. You know that organizations aggressively seek out these top performers as the rarest commodity. However, there are some core problems with this approach of raiding your competitors and others for exceptional talent. First, as noted earlier, there simply isn't enough raw talent to go around. Second, hiring and retraining high-profile talent is costly. However, the biggest risk is that talented people do not always produce the results expected!

Think about it. Do you know any truly talented people who have underachieved in their careers? These are the people who bring significant potential to the table, but perform at or below an established standard. Why? Because talent is a measure of the potential to perform, not of performance. Businesses do not succeed because they have potential. They succeed because they produce results. Let me state this in a different way. People with high potential (the capacity to succeed) don't drive successful companies. Rather, successful companies are driven by people who routinely accomplish exceptional results.

Talent is a measure of the potential to perform, not of performance. Businesses do not succeed because they have potential, but because they produce results.

The stars who make such a significant difference in our businesses are those individuals who have the potential to succeed *and* make the effort to improve in their roles day in and day out. The implications of this are staggering for those of us who manage individuals, teams, departments, divisions, and companies. If variance in the performance of people and teams is not determined simply by the raw talent you have acquired, then.... *Leadership has the ability to shift the performance curve.*

We need to move our focus from inputs (talent, potential, competencies) to the outputs that matter (revenue, accomplishments, customer retention, and so forth). Please note two important caveats here:

- Actions and activities are not outputs.
- Level of activity (how busy someone is) does not equate to success any more than raw talent does.

If you asked your COO or divisional VP about the types of employees they value the most, what do you suspect would be their choice from the options below?

- Employees who knew more, had greater skills and competencies, and scored higher on relevant tests
- Employees who were busy all the time
- Employees who consistently produced outstanding results that drove the corporate strategy and initiatives

Having asked these questions scores of times, our experience indicates that across industries, functions, and levels, from supervisors to the COO, the third response is consistently the dominant choice. It makes sense that business leaders care more about actual business results than about the potential to perform. People need to have the capability to perform (skills, knowledge, and so on) in order to excel at their work. Yet having the capability is not sufficient to produce superior results.

Activity Versus Accomplishment

In his 1996 book *Human Competence*, Thomas Gilbert argued for a shift in focus in order to produce effective performance improvement: focus on what people produce in the work environment, not simply on what they do.[6] Helping workers more efficiently perform tasks that don't produce the desired accomplishments does not improve a company's performance. Instead, you need to focus on and identify what a worker's major accomplishments are up front and then determine how those accomplishments contribute to the company's business goals. Once you have this information, you can determine the tasks and support systems needed for workers to produce those accomplishments with a high level of competence and confidence.

Figure 1.3 illustrates Gilbert's point. The first column on the left represents what the organization provides to support an individual or team in their performance. The next column

Figure 1.3. Accomplishments Versus Behavior

Influences	Behavior	Accomplishments	Goals
Skills/ knowledge	Sell products	Revenues	Profits
Motivation	Make decisions	Plans	High returns
Supportive environment	Diagnose problems	Delighted customers	Customer satisfaction

Performance **unfolds** in this direction ⟶

⟵ We **analyze** in this direction

Source: Exemplary Performance, LLC.

represents the actions or tasks that individuals execute based on the influences provided by the organization. The third column from the left represents the accomplishments or results that are produced as a result of the actions that are performed. The column on the far right represents the goals that are supported by those accomplishments or results. When we think about performance, we see the process unfolding from left to right.

However, if the purpose is to improve performance, the analysis must move from right to left. By starting with the goals or strategy of the organization, you begin the process with a focus on which accomplishments are most critical to execute and achieve the organization's strategy and goals. This knowledge enables you to capture the critical tasks required to produce those accomplishments, as well as identify those actions and activities that are not contributing directly to the desired results. Once the required actions or tasks are determined, then the work allocating organizational support is the natural follow-on step.

It is important to notice that costs are incurred in the left two columns and value is produced in the right two columns. That is to say, no matter how elaborate the interventions and how busy the people are, if no accomplishments are produced, *no value has accrued to the organization!*

Creating Profiles of Exemplary Performance

The most effective and efficient way to capture models of optimal performance is to work with your current stars. These are the individuals who have established approaches to their work that consistently produce the desired accomplishments at a routinely high level. You can think of these exemplary performers as internal benchmarks. They are currently operating within the same organizational structure and culture as the rest of your employees, yet these individuals have found ways to exceed your organization's expectations.

Exemplary performers are often unconsciously competent!

One of the most interesting aspects of identifying exemplary performers is that these individuals are often unconsciously competent! They can't provide clear explanations for their success or what they do differently to produce outstanding results. In fact, when asked, these performers may give inaccurate or vague explanations. Many times these individuals have developed rich mental models of what success looks like and developed ways of predicting a successful outcome. Frequently, we find these exemplary performers don't share their approaches or methodologies because they assume that what they do is not that unusual.

Decades of experience have allowed us to refine a process for capturing this hidden expertise (see Chapter Four). *We have learned that asking stars why they are good at what they do or how they go about doing their work is always unsuccessful.* It is only through observation, interviews, and deep case-based analysis that we are able to capture reliable answers.

For example, if you're working with a project manager and want to capture his or her expertise, it is best to ask him or her to walk you through one or more recent projects from beginning to end while asking such questions as:

- What did you consider when producing the project plan and work breakdown structure?
- What resources did you tap when deciding on project staffing?
- Have you developed any tools to address particular components of the project management process?
- What is it in your environment that enabled you to be successful?

Similarly, if analyzing a sales role, you might do a deep analysis of one or more of the significant wins of an individual salesperson or sales team. This approach to capturing a model of optimal performance allows you to identify what specifically is required to be a superstar.

Here's a tangible example: A number of years ago we were working with a major automotive manufacturer. At the time, the company was in the process of installing a new paint booth in one of their assembly plants. The equipment vendor had been tasked with delivering training to the operators and to those who would maintain the new technology. Now, as often is the case, the training was designed by the design engineering staff of the paint booth manufacturer. This made a lot of sense from the vendor's perspective, because the engineers knew the intricacies of the booth they had designed.

We were asked to review the training that the equipment supplier had provided. The training included a four-hour module on the viscosity of paints that both the booth operators and the technical maintenance workers were required to take. Clearly, requiring expertise in the viscosity of paints made sense for the design engineering staff, because one of their outputs was the nozzle design. However, all that the operators needed to know was how to adjust the paint booth controls in order to produce their output—vehicles with a high-quality finish. An in-depth understanding of paint viscosity would have no impact on the accomplishment of a high-quality vehicle finish.

This is a simple example, but it illustrates the relationship between the strategy and goals of an organization and what elements are needed for success. It's all about the accomplishments required to achieve the business result (vehicles with a high-quality finish), the tasks that must be implemented to produce those results (adjust the paint booth controls), and support systems and tools that the organization must provide to help people succeed. It gives us a mechanism for taking a truly "lean" approach to improving performance.

Figure 1.4 illustrates the value of shifting the performance curve between good and best performers. The implications are significant. By producing greater results (vehicles with a high-quality finish, sales, customer satisfaction/retention, and so forth) with the existing workforce and resources, a significant percentage of the value of improved performance falls directly to the bottom line. The shaded area of the curve represents this increase in results.

Here is another example: Let's say that you have a sales force of 400 people carrying a quota of $1,000,000. The best salespeople are generating $1,500,000 in revenue. You analyze the performance of these sales stars and develop a model, based on their proven practices, which you want to transfer to the rest of the sales force. If you implement a performance architecture based on your current stars, you can close the gap by 20% ($100,000), skewing the curve to the right. The shaded area of

Figure 1.4. Shifting the Performance Curve

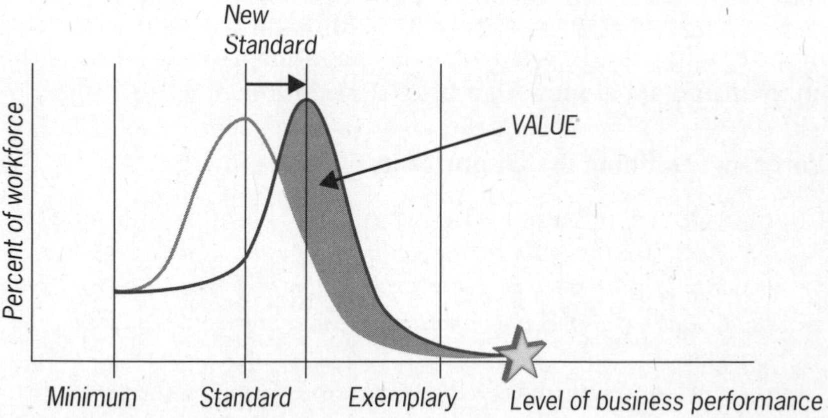

Source: Exemplary Performance, LLC.

the curve equates to an increase in revenue of approximately $40,000,000. This is the potential of internal benchmarking to enhance business results.

Summary: The Value Proposition for This Book

For more than twenty-five years, we have helped organizations reach their goals by leveraging the insights of their star performers. We've done this by shifting the performance curve and successfully replicating the performance of stars. This method has proved successful across multiple industries such as telecommunications, financial services, automotive, pharmaceutical, and high technology. Most of the readers of this book are likely leaders and managers whose most critical output is to produce and lead high-performing individuals and teams. This book will enable you to be an exemplary performer in your role as leader and provide you with the models required so that you can shift the performance curve for your own department, team, or organization.

The book is structured in two parts. The first part will equip you to prioritize your efforts, identify your true stars or exemplars, and create models of optimal performance for critical roles within your organization. The second part will equip you to be the architect of the requisite systems required to shift the performance curve by leveraging the insights of your star performers. Here is the chapter line-up, along with a brief description:

Part One: Defining the Opportunity

Chapter One: The Value of Leveraging the Insights of Your Stars
This is a synopsis of the value proposition for leveraging the insights of your stars in order to shift the performance curve to the right. It also describes the importance of moving your focus from talent to results.

Chapter Two: Prioritizing Performance Improvement Opportunities
Given limited resources, this will help you establish priorities based on potential impact.

Chapter Three: Selecting Exemplary Teams and Individuals
You'll find an objective approach to distinguishing between perceived "stars" and real "stars." This will also explain why we so often get this wrong.

Chapter Four: Capturing the Expertise of Your Stars
Once you have identified your stars, this will provide a methodology for capturing their unconscious competence and create Profiles of Exemplary Performance.

Chapter Five: What Makes Them Tick? How Stars and Exemplary Teams Consistently Exceed Expectations
We share some common characteristics we have seen in star performers across industries and roles.

Part Two: Shifting the Performance Curve

Chapter Six: Leading for Exceptional Results
Introducing Part Two, this chapter describes the role of leadership in enabling high performance. It stresses the basic need to align the multiple influences that can support or inhibit high performance.

Chapter Seven: You Get What You Expect and What You Inspect
The ability to provide clear, objective expectations with targeted, timely feedback is the fundamental requirement for managers who want to produce stars.

Chapter Eight: Great Job! Rewards, Recognition, and Consequences

You can never use punishment to produce stars! Instead, here is guidance on identifying and leveraging recognition and rewards for shifting the performance curve.

Chapter Nine: How to Succeed in Business by Really Trying: Motivation, Intentionality, and Deliberate Practice

Where did we ever get the idea that stars succeed based on innate ability alone? It simply doesn't work that way!

Chapter Ten: Replicating Your Stars! Training and Performance Support

Here we address training, readiness, and performance support. You need to ensure that your folks can access the right information exactly when they need it. We also address where information should be stored to allow for efficient and effective retrieval.

Chapter Eleven: Getting Round Pegs in the Round Holes: Selecting for Success

Hiring the right people and assigning employees to the right roles is critical. We provide an accomplishment-based model for ensuring job fit.

Chapter Twelve: Creating Barrier-Free Work Systems

Organizational design, job design, and process design—when done well, these allow for optimal performance. If done poorly, they are significant barriers to high performance.

Epilogue: Just Imagine . . .

What would it look like if you designed a barrier-free, high-performing work environment and your team's performance curve shifted optimally to the right?

———

Keep reading. You're on your way to driving the business results that your organization requires by leveraging the insights of your star performers. Expect incredible results!

Notes
1. Geoff Colvin, *Talent Is Overrated: What Really Separates World-Class Performers from Everybody Else* (New York: Portfolio, 2008).
2. Ibid., 66.

3. Ibid., 63.
4. *Merriam-Webster Dictionary.* Retrieved November, 2011, from http://www.merriam-webster.com/dictionary.
5. Geary Rummler and Alan Brache, *Improving Performance: Managing the White Space on the Organizational Chart* (San Francisco: Jossey-Bass, 1995), 13.
6. T. F. Gilbert, *Human Competence: Engineering Worthy Performance* (Amherst, MA: HRD Press, 1996).

CHAPTER TWO

Prioritizing Performance Improvement Opportunities

In This Chapter

- A "Target Rich" Environment
- Determining Priorities: Alignment with Strategy
- Determining Priorities: The Variance in Current Performance
- Determining Priorities: Estimating the Potential Impact
- Scoping the Improvement Initiative

A "Target Rich" Environment

Based on the alternative approach provided in Chapter One and our experience, we hope it has become clear that most organizations provide a "target rich" environment for your performance improvement efforts. By now you may have concluded that there is significant upside potential to be achieved if you can leverage the insight of your stars and shift the performance curve; it's just a question of where to begin.

Imagine the possibilities if you and your organization acted on the premise that the talent curve does *not* predetermine the performance curve. If you were able to measure the gap between the results of your star performers and the results of your solid, but average performers, what would you find? You'd first discover that the difference is astounding—with the value potentially running in the scores of millions of dollars, particularly if you are looking across multiple roles. Moreover, suppose you were able to move those average performers closer toward star status, closing the gap by 20, 30, or even 40%. The results for your company would be game changing, and you would be seen as the star for driving value!

This chapter will help you navigate this "target rich" environment by providing a rationale for prioritizing your improvement initiatives. To do this, you will first need to:

- Identify the roles most critical to executing your business strategy.
- Determine the variance in performance for incumbents in these critical roles.
- Estimate the impact of decreasing this variance.

Determining Priorities: Alignment with Strategy

Today's leaders must be able to take the strategy they set for their organizations and turn it into results. One of the most effective ways to achieve this is to leverage the insights of your current exemplary performers, who already contribute significantly to implementing your strategy.

Organizations face many challenges today—competitive battles, increased costs, decreased margins, and a variety of other internal and external forces. It is critical, in response to these challenges, to turn your strategic goals into measurable results. One of the most effective ways to achieve this is to leverage the insights of your current exemplary performers, who already contribute significantly to implementing your strategy and do so within your current culture and work systems.

Unfortunately, too many companies struggle to bridge the gap between strategy and results. By that we mean that they create solid, logical, and even bold plans, but find they are unable to properly execute them. It is the rare company that includes leveraging the insights of their stars as a critical component of effectively implementing their strategic plans.

Clearly, great organizations understand that an exemplary workforce is absolutely essential to executing strategy. General Electric, IBM, and Microsoft all have well-developed systems for managing and motivating their high-potential and, *ideally*, high-performing employees. These and many other companies around the world focus on their A-players (and there is certainly merit and logic to this approach). However, if you focus exclusively on your A-players without identifying your A-positions, you randomize your organization's performance improvement initiatives. You create the possibility that your organization's highest performers may not be assigned to the roles most critical for the execution of your strategy. This may seem obvious, but it's surprising how few companies systematically identify their strategically important A-positions before finding the high performers to fill them. It's a business practice that's much harder to implement than it is to state. The most successful businesses improve their performance by:

- Placing their exceptional employees in strategic positions;
- Placing solid performers in support positions; and
- Either eliminating nonperforming employees or placing them in essential, but less critical jobs.

Traditionally, the value of a job in an organization is assessed in one of two ways. Human resource professionals look at the level of skill, effort, and responsibility a job entails. The most important positions are those held by the most highly skilled individuals who exercise the most responsibility and who work in the hardest, most challenging environments.

Economists, by contrast, generally believe that people's wages reflect the value they create for the company and the relative scarcity of their skills in the labor market. Thus, the most important jobs are those held by the most highly paid employees. Unfortunately, our experience and practice tell us that these approaches do not really identify the most important jobs. They merely describe jobs that the company is currently treating as most important.

To find the truly important jobs, you need to be working *forward* from the organizational strategy, not *backwards* from organizational charts or compensation systems. In other words, it is the strategy that determines which are A-positions and not the organizational chart or compensation model. That's why we advocate that the two defining characteristics of A-positions should be

- How critically important a job is to the company's capacity to execute its strategy and
- How much variance exists in the quality of the work displayed among the current employees in these critical positions.

Clearly, to determine a position's strategic significance, you first must be clear about your company's strategy. You have to answer the question of strategic competitive differentiators in your company before asking what jobs are critical to the execution of this strategy. What you will find is that such positions are as variable as the strategies they promote.

It's Not Just About Org Charts

The key point we want to make is that no inherently strategic positions exist simply as defined by the organizational chart and that these clearly strategic positions—less than 20% of the workforce—are likely to be scattered throughout the organization. That's why you will increase the probability of effectively executing your strategy if you identify critical jobs and then invest disproportionately to shift the performance curve for those roles.

It's important to emphasize that A-positions are not directly tied to a firm's hierarchy, which is the common default often used to identify roles with the greatest opportunity for impact. Remember that A-positions are found throughout an organization and may be relatively simple jobs that are, nonetheless, essential to your company's unique strategy.

In an article entitled "A Players or A Positions? The Strategic Logic of Workforce Management," Huselid, Beatty, and Becker described the following case: A major pharmaceutical firm was trying to identify the jobs that had a high impact on the implementation of the company's strategy and in the process identified several A-positions.[1] Because the company's ability to test the safety and efficacy of its products was a strategic capability, it identified as critical positions the head of clinical trials, as well as a number of positions in the regulatory affairs office. However, some top jobs in the company hierarchy, including the director of manufacturing and the corporate treasurer, were not judged as critical. Although people in these jobs were highly compensated, made important decisions, and played key roles in maintaining the company's value, they were not core to the firm's business model nor did the employees in these positions provide significant competitive differentiation.

Consequently, the company chose not to make substantial investments in these leadership positions and concentrated more of its performance improvement dollars in the strategic jobs within research and development.

Right People, Right Jobs

The ultimate aim of our approach to prioritization is to help you manage your portfolio of positions so that the right people are in the right jobs, while paying particular attention to those who occupy A-positions. You do this by first using performance criteria based on your particular model of star performance. Then you calculate the percentage of A-players, B-players, and C-players currently occupying A-positions in your organization. Then the math is simple: you act quickly to get C-players out of A-positions and work just as quickly to shift the performance of any B-players in these critical positions to more closely replicate the performance of your stars.

In their book *Execution*, Honeywell CEO Larry Bossidy and management advisor Ram Charan contend that the reason for the gap between strategy and execution is that businesspeople do not think about execution as a discipline.[2] From middle management all the way up to the CEO, a company's leaders must recognize execution as the most important collective set of activities in which they engage.

From the Field, for the Field

We are advocating an approach to execution that is not crafted in the board room and pushed out to operations, but rather is "captured" from your star performers, currently located throughout your enterprise, and then infused into the performance of the organization's larger population of solid performers. We regularly see how this approach leads to a real "pull" from the field, as employees recognize that new approaches and practices are based on the performance of their highly regarded peers. This recognition of and respect for these "homegrown" practices creates an environment that encourages emulation among the solid performers. A sales organization, with whom we have worked for over a decade, refers to the results of our work as "from the field, for the field."

Optimizing the performance of people is core to implementing strategy and operations; if you don't get the people process right, you will never fulfill the potential of your business. A people-centric execution process does several essential things:

- It provides absolute clarity around the relationship between each individual's role and the overall success of the organization of which he or she is a part. We refer to this as each contributor being aware of *the worth of his or her work.*
- It defines success in that role in terms of measurable outputs or accomplishments, not simply activities. The accomplishments are not only defined, but the excellence indicators or metrics are provided in terms of quality, quantity, timeliness, and so on.
- It provides each individual with constructive feedback in a timely manner. It doesn't assume that the individual is the problem—it explores broader system barriers to achieving the desired results. If the feedback has identified gaps in performance, it also provides a path forward to improve that performance.
- It recognizes and rewards high performance and provides for remediation of both the people and systems when performance does not meet expectations.

In today's execution-focused companies, human capital must be seamlessly integrated into the business process. It must be linked to strategy and operations, and to employee assessments across the enterprise. This strategic and operational link means that HR professionals are expected to have a point of view about how to achieve business objectives or implement the strategic plan. Consequently, business acumen, critical thinking skills, and the ability to link strategy and execution are expected competencies of today's HR professional. In other words, they must have the same strategic skills as any business leader.

A good strategic planning process requires that careful attention be paid to how the strategy is executed. A robust strategy is not simply a compilation of numbers, nor is it a "crystal ball" used to forecast growth for the next ten years. It is an action plan that business leaders can rely on.

This means that your action plan must:

- Identify and define the critical issues behind your strategy.
- Review the basic assumptions of your strategy.
- Determine whether you have the organizational capability to execute the plan.
- Determine whether your strategy links to your people processes (that is, whether you have the right people in place to execute the strategy) and to your operating plan (to get your organization properly aligned to move forward).

We believe the operating plan should address a prioritized list of roles where you want to shift the performance curve.

The operating plan provides the detailed path for the people responsible for execution by breaking out long-term results into short-term targets. An operating plan also includes the programs (product launches, marketing plan, sales plan, and so forth) that your business expects to complete within one year to reach the desired business metrics (earnings, sales, margins, and cash flow). In addition, we believe the operating plan should address a prioritized list of roles where you want to shift the performance curve.

Of course, the assumptions on which the operating plan is based are linked to the situational reality that has been debated by both the financial professionals who provide the business parameters and line leaders who must execute the approved plan. You, as the leader, are just one of a number of stakeholders who construct the plan, even though you must be intimately familiar with all the processes involved in executing the strategy.

Not only does this inclusive process engender buy-in, but it ensures that all the moving parts of the organization have a common understanding of the external environment and other crucial factors that are part of the strategy. Synchronizing and linking the goals of the interdependent parts of the plan with other parts of the organization also ensures that, when conditions change, synchronization realigns the multiple priorities and properly reallocates resources.

Shifting the performance curve for the people in A-positions creates substantial competitive advantage that warrants the attention of leaders at the highest level.

An organization's workers are its most reliable resource for generating excellent results year after year. Their judgment, experience, and capabilities make the difference between success and failure. Yet, it remains a puzzle why the same leaders who say that "people are our most important asset" often don't perceive the link between choosing the right people for the right jobs and their ultimate success. Typically, this is because most leaders are focused on the big picture—how to make their companies bigger or better positioned globally—and not this critical issue of allocating people resources. We believe that shifting the performance curve for the people in A-positions creates substantial competitive advantage that warrants the attention of leaders at the highest level.

Why, then, are the right people not in the right jobs? Leaders often rely on sometimes fuzzy or prejudiced staff appraisals for job placement, rather than first defining the job itself in terms of its critical accomplishments or results. We believe that this clarification of job accomplishments is essential *before* thinking about staffing the job with people who will consistently produce those specific results at an exceptional level.

A second important issue is the willingness of leaders to address substandard performance directly. Often, leaders don't have the emotional fortitude to take decisive action to remove the wrong person in a job. In other cases, the leader may simply be comfortable with certain people in certain roles or feel loyal to an individual performer. This can cause the leader to ignore poor job fit. Such failures to take action (whether the reasons are social or professional) do considerable damage to a business. And interestingly, breaking free of this comfort factor is exactly what a leader must do to bring about change.

Once you have identified these A-positions, the focus of our approach is on ensuring that the individuals and teams in these critical roles demonstrate exemplary performance. This is achieved by determining the factors that differentiate high and low performance in each position. With these specific factors determined, it is possible to measure against these criteria and take steps to make sure that the standards are met or exceeded.

Determining Priorities: The Variance in Current Performance

Once we have identified the A-positions that provide the greatest strategic leverage, why would variability in the performance of incumbents be so important? Because variation in performance represents upside potential— *shifting the performance curve to the right in these critical roles will pay huge dividends*. Furthermore, if your competitors have similar variance in these critical roles, and they most probably do, shifting your company's performance curve to the right will be a source of significant competitive advantage.

Why Variance Is Important

A simple illustration might further illuminate the importance of variation and its impact on improved performance. Suppose you were a coach at your local swim club and were working with five-, six-, and seven-year-olds. The lap time across members of your team would likely vary by tens of seconds. As you worked with these young swimmers during the season, you would hope to see two shifts in performance occur; the top speed of your best swimmers would improve and the gap across the swimmers would narrow. It's quite possible that this would occur even with only two or three coaching sessions per week. The large variance in initial performance allows for rapid improvement with minimal investment.

In contrast, think of Michael Phelps. During the 2008 summer Olympics, he won his seventh Olympic gold medal in the

100-meter butterfly. He accomplished this by setting an Olympic record for the event with a time of 50.58 seconds and edging out his nearest competitor, Milorad Cavic, by 1/100th of a second. The level of investment it takes to shave 1/100th of a second off the time of an Olympic-level athlete is enormous and would likely take a year of intense practice. In contrast to the junior swimmers, the minimal variance in performance at this level requires massive investment for scant improvement. This same principle applies when you are looking for the best place to invest your performance improvement resources within your organization.

Sales positions, fundamental to the success of many a company's strategy, are a good case in point. A salesperson whose performance is in the 85th percentile of a company's sales staff frequently generates two to three times the revenue of someone in the 50th percentile. But we're not just talking about greater or lesser value creation; *we're also talking about the potential for value creation versus value destruction.*

The Gallup organization, for instance, surveyed 45,000 customers of a company known for customer service, to evaluate its customer service representatives. The reps' performance ranged widely. The top quartile of workers had a positive effect on 61% of the customers they talked to, the second 40%, the third quartile just 27%. The bottom quartile actually had, as a group, a negative effect on customers. These customer service workers were actually destroying value by alienating customers.

The real significance of this example is the huge difference that improving the performance of the subpar reps makes to these organizations. Imagine if the managers focused on these poorly performing reps, whether through intensive training, more careful screening of the people hired for the role, or reassigning or replacing ill-suited reps. Clearly, this company's performance would improve tremendously.

In contrast, some jobs may be important strategically, but currently represent little opportunity for competitive advantage because everyone's performance is already at a high level. That may either be because of the standardized nature of the job or because a company or industry has, through hiring and training, reduced the variability and increased the mean performance of workers to a point at which further investment isn't merited. For example,

A job must meet the dual criteria of strategic impact and performance variability if it is to qualify as a logical place to invest your performance improvement resources.

commercial pilots are a key contributor to the airlines' strategic goal of safety. However, due to recurrent training throughout the pilots' careers and government regulations, there is little variance between the performance of these professionals. Although there definitely is a downside if the performance of some pilots were to degrade, significantly improving pilot performance is unlikely and, even if marginal gains are possible, these changes are unlikely to provide an opportunity for competitive advantage. The point is that a job must meet the dual criteria of strategic impact and performance variability if it is to qualify as a logical place to invest your performance improvement resources.

Determining Priorities: Estimating the Potential Impact

What would be the impact on your company if you closed the gap between average performers and star performers by 20%, 30%, or 40%? We will provide you with an alternative on how you can drive greater business results by leveraging exemplary performers throughout your organization. Simply put, by shifting the performance curve, you automatically:

- Drive results
- Enhance revenue
- Improve margins

This alternative allows organizations, their leaders, and associated work teams to capture more value with existing resources. In today's "do more with less" economy, this is an approach that will clearly differentiate you from your competition.

As you recall from Chapter One, our approach depends on the clear identification of the key accomplishments or outputs produced by an individual or team. The value proposition for improving performance is tied to improvements in the quality, cost, or timeliness of those accomplishments.

Therefore, it is necessary to look at the critical A-positions that you have identified, estimate or guesstimate the variance that exists within each of those positions, and calculate the potential value of shifting the performance curve for those positions.

Focusing on accomplishments or results is essential. As Figure 2.1 indicates, a lot of what individual workers know and a lot of what they do falls outside of the band of value-added knowledge and activity. You must analyze from right to left—from outputs to actions to knowledge—to ensure that you are focusing your performance improvement resources on what really matters. *Without this accomplishment focus*, resources can be poured into helping workers get really good at what doesn't matter. In addition, you may supply them with a lot of useless information.

> Without this accomplishment focus, *resources can be poured into helping workers get really good at what doesn't matter.*

An Example

Here is a simple example that may help explain the importance of this concept. Imagine you are responsible for a customer contact center with a team of 200 customer service representatives (CSRs).

Figure 2.1. A Paradigm Shift—From Knowledge to Results

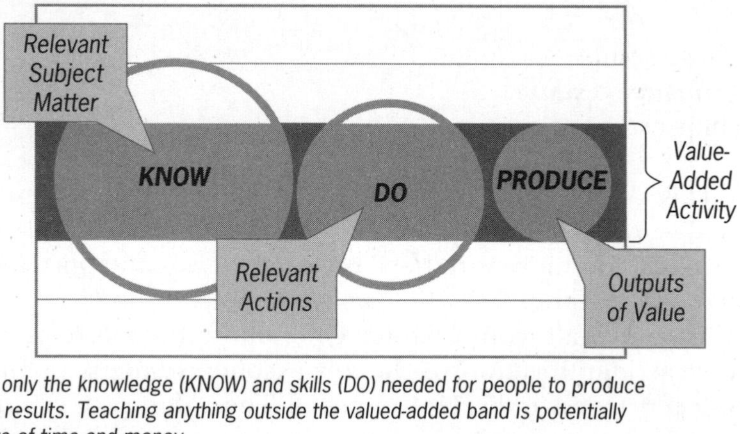

KNOW   DO   PRODUCE

Relevant Subject Matter

Relevant Actions

Outputs of Value

Value-Added Activity

Teach only the knowledge (KNOW) and skills (DO) needed for people to produce valued results. Teaching anything outside the valued-added band is potentially a waste of time and money.

Source: Exemplary Performance, LLC.

The goal for each team member is to upsell each inbound phone call by 15% or $6.00, given that the average initial order size is $40. Currently, the average upsell is 8%, far below the goal. In contrast, your 12 best performers have an average upsell of 22%. The last piece of data is that on a typical day the contact center handles 12,000 inbound phone calls.

One major accomplishment for each CSR, therefore, is $6.00 in enhanced revenue per call. The actual additional revenue per call is $3.20. In contrast, the exemplary performers are producing an additional $8.80 per call. There is incredible potential value to the company. How? By leveraging the expertise of those 12 stars and improving the performance of the other 188 CSRs, so that they increase the average revenue per call by $2.80, multiplied times the 11,280 calls handled by the average CSRs. *This equates to $31,584 per day in enhanced revenue with zero additional costs to the contact center.*

So at a high level, here is the process for estimating the potential value of your performance improvement opportunities:

1. Compile a list of those roles within your organization that
    1.1 Align closely with your strategic intent; and
    1.2 Exhibit a high degree of variability in performance across role incumbents.
2. Identify one or more major accomplishments for each critical role on your list. By the way, this can be a more challenging activity than you may expect.
3. Review the best available data on the current variance in performance.
4. Estimate the percentage by which you can reduce that variance.
5. Calculate the value of shifting the performance curve to the right by the estimated amount.

Another Example

The previous example provided a quick overview of the process, but here's a more comprehensive one. Imagine you are the executive vice president for Annapolis Manufacturing, Inc., and you are in the business of producing automotive components for customers across North America. Your business strategy focuses on being the most reliable just-in-time, error-free components supplier to your main customer base, which is automotive assembly plants.

The leadership team at Annapolis Manufacturing wants to identify the most critical roles that enhance this competitive position. Part of the reason for this decision is the discovery that costs are rising within both the manufacturing and distribution divisions and margins are degrading. A team is assembled to analyze the problem and generate possible solutions. The team decides to use the process we described previously as a way of prioritizing their efforts.

The first step in the process is to identify positions in the company that are absolutely essential to executing Annapolis Manufacturing's strategy. Three roles are identified: plant manager, account manager, and distribution manager. Team members scurry around looking for evidence of variability within those roles. They find out that there is little variance evidenced in the distribution side of the company. However, significant variance in unit costs exists across the plants. The team also notes that the amount of overtime used varies significantly from plant to plant.

On the sales side, the team discovers a variance in quota attainment and, surprisingly, major variance in forecast accuracy—way beyond their expectations. One of the team members hypothesizes that there may be a relationship between the accuracy of forecasts and the overtime used by the plants. One of the team members is assigned to explore this potential interaction more closely.

Identify Accomplishments

The team then takes time to clearly identify the major accomplishments for the two roles exhibiting high variability. For the plant manager, two critical accomplishments were identified:

- Overtime costs
- Production schedules

For account managers, three accomplishments were identified:

- Contracts that meet or exceed quota
- Retained customers
- Forecasts

Next, the team explores the degree of variance exhibited for each of those accomplishments. For the plant managers, it was clear that a significant variance in overtime costs and in the accuracy of production schedules exists. However, two of the 12 plants showed significantly less overtime and seemed to be able to gauge production requirements with a high degree of accuracy.

For the account managers, customer retention was high across the board. And since the new VP of sales had joined the company five years ago, all of the account managers were consistently meeting or exceeding quota. Unfortunately, the accuracy of the forecasts submitted by the sales force varied widely. Four of the account managers consistently submitted forecasts that were accurate within plus or minus 5%. The other 30 account managers would submit forecasts that were off by 30% to 50% or more.

Forecasting Accuracy

When the team member who was exploring the relationship between forecast accuracy and overtime costs returned with her report, the evidence supported the fact that inaccurate forecasts corresponded directly with the excessive use of overtime. The team also noticed that the most cost-effective plants were those being supported by the account managers with the accurate forecasts. With this information in hand, the team decided to focus initially on improving forecast accuracy. The evidence indicated that if all the account managers had forecasts that were accurate within plus or minus 7%, overtime could be reduced by 40% and this, in turn, would improve margins by 3%, or approximately $3,200,000.

Following this step-by-step process enabled Annapolis Manufacturing to clearly prioritize where to focus their performance improvement resources. It also allowed the company to gain an early win in using the approach advocated in this book, which garnered support for applying it more widely.

Scoping the Improvement Initiative

Keeping the preceding detailed example in mind, here's an example of how you would take the next step in the process— scoping the improvement initiative.

The following table provides a high-level process flow, with a typical range of effort for each major activity in the initiative. This will provide enough information to allow you to roughly estimate the resources required to implement one of these projects within your own organization.

Admittedly, this table can only help you generate a gross estimate of the level of effort involved. However, it will be close enough to allow you to approximate the benefit-to-cost ratio.

Table 2.1. Scoping the Project for Annapolis Manufacturing

Task	Range of Hours Per Task	Number of Iterations	Average Hours
Project Initiation	16–32	1	16–32
Review of Documentation	16–32	1	16–32
Stakeholder Interviews	1–2	Number of Stakeholders	24–48
Interview of Star Performers	2–4	Number of Star Performers	60–120
Synthesis of Results; Report Generation	40–60	1	40–60
Design of High-Performing Work System	80–240	1	80–240
Development of Work System	?	1	?
System Implementation	?	1	?

In this hypothetical example, the anticipated benefit would be $3,200,000. The anticipated cost would fall between $200,000 and $300,000. Though clearly these are hypothetical approximations, this would produce an ROI of just over 1,000%. Talk about driving business results!

Our experience indicates that substantial intangible benefits are derived from these types of initiatives. We believe strongly that stakeholders and other employees are enthusiastic about contributing to the success of their organizations. We routinely see intangibles such as improved job satisfaction, increased organizational commitment or engagement, enhanced teamwork, and higher customer satisfaction as a result of the performance improvement approach we are presenting.

Summary

This chapter provided you with an approach for establishing priorities for your performance improvement efforts. The next chapter provides the requisite steps to clearly identify your exemplary performers—both individuals and teams—within the targeted roles. As exemplary performers in your organization come to mind, make notes to yourself. There's no better time than NOW to begin driving business results by leveraging your star performers!

Notes
1. M. A. Huselid, R. W. Beatty, and B. E. Becker, "A Players or A Positions? The Strategic Logic of Workforce Management," *Harvard Business Review Online* (December 2005).
2. L. Bossidy and R. Charan, *Execution* (New York: Crown Business, 2002).

CHAPTER THREE

Selecting Exemplary Teams and Individuals

In This Chapter

- Deciding Whether to Focus on Individual or Team Accomplishments
- Selecting Your Exemplary Performers
- Creating "Synthetic" Exemplary Performers
- Validation of Exemplary Performer Selection

In Chapter Two, you read about prioritizing where to invest your time and attention within your organization. In general, we want to focus our efforts where we will achieve the greatest return on investment. We have narrowed our focus to those roles or functions with the greatest upside potential, based on metrics that make sense within your particular organization. The next step is to determine whether we will concentrate on an individual role or focus on team performance. The question becomes: "Do individuals or teams produce the critical accomplishments that provide value to the organization?"

As you begin your investigation, keep in mind that your search for the real source of accomplishment has three possibilities:

- Stars who are individual contributors;
- Exemplary performers who are members of high-performing teams; or
- Managers of clusters of stars; our experience shows that when you encounter a cluster of stars, it is likely their manager is the true exemplar that you will want to replicate.

Deciding Whether to Focus on Individual or Team Accomplishments

On some level, deciding whether a team or an individual is primarily responsible for valued accomplishments is a very straightforward decision. For example, when salespeople set up appointments, make their own calls, have one-on-one discussions with potential clients, and are individually responsible for closing the deal, it's easy to say the individual role should be the focus of any ensuing analysis. In the case of an "outside operator" at an oil refinery, who just happens to work the second shift along with three other workers, determining individual or team responsibility may at first appear more difficult.

For outside operators, each worker has clear responsibilities with little overlap. Although they do work as a team and can rely on one another for specific tasks, closer examination reveals that their *job outputs* are their own. Here again, the focus of the analysis is on the individual role and we look for individual exemplary performers. Though most people accomplish their work in some type of team setting, it is the outputs of individuals that most commonly provide value to the organization.

Another way to look at the issue of individual versus team accomplishment is to examine responsibilities and accountabilities. Is there an individual charged with producing certain reports, closing a deal, or returning a piece of machinery to working order following a breakdown? If so, then your focus will be at the individual role level.

When you encounter a cluster of stars, it is likely their manager is the true exemplar that you will want to replicate.

On the other hand, if the valued accomplishments are truly produced by a team, the source of these accomplishments may be the manager of the team who is responsible and accountable for the team results. In such cases, it will be very apparent that the output focus is on the manager or supervisor of the exemplary team.

Another clue in a search for the real source of valued accomplishments is often uncovered by examining data about star performers. Sometimes star performers are found in "clusters" in the organization, and it is this clustering that leads to the hypothesis that the manager is the exemplary performer whose output is high-performing direct reports. Once star managers are uncovered, you can examine what these managers are doing to obtain such great results.

Still, the real source of team or individual results is not always obvious in the real world. Sometimes retail managers regard all store employees as part of a team. In other cases, all department heads in a corporate situation are regarded as a cohesive and responsible management team. Thus, asking the right questions is vitally important in these situations.

For example, to really ascertain the source of high performance in a large grocery chain, you might ask various department managers how involved they were in the success of other departments (for example, did any deli department actions drive significant results in the grocery department?). Or, to put the example in the language of process management, do the outputs of one department become the inputs to another department?

Sometimes the answer to whether we should remain focused on individuals or shift to a team focus is not clear until individual star performers are identified and we begin to understand how they accomplish their work.

Clearly, a surgeon is not solely responsible for the successful outcome of a surgical procedure. Yet we recognize that some surgeons have significantly better results than others. You could envision a scenario that plays out in which we first identify the most successful surgeons and then conduct some preliminary interviews.

You could ask an exemplary surgeon about her mental model for what she considers a valued accomplishment and hear something like: "*A post-surgical outcome that allows the patient to resume all normal work and family activities with the shortest recovery time possible.*"

As you review surgical cases and interview exemplary surgeons, you repeatedly hear about the contributions of the intake nurse, the preoperative team, actions by other team members in the operating room (anesthesiologist, nurses), and those who provide postoperative care. In scenarios such as this, we focus on the team accomplishments versus individual accomplishments and our quest to identify star performers shifts to the team level. We ask which surgical *teams* consistently produce the desired results (accomplishments) at or above the established standards and criteria.

In complex sales projects, we have frequently found that the first priority is to assemble a high-performing team. Or, rather, we observe that the star performers are consistently part of high-performing teams. The defining aspect is that the team accomplishment is not achievable by one person alone; critical handoffs occur among team members and individual accomplishments contribute to the valued team accomplishment.

What Are Relevant Performance Data?

Here are some pointers for understanding which data are most relevant and important to a particular organization.

- In some high-growth industries the most important metrics may be year-over-year revenue growth.
- Some organizations have very stable and predictable costs and gross revenue is the key indicator of success.
- Other organizations put an emphasis on controlling costs, in addition to increasing revenue.

Finding All the Stars

As noted earlier, while investigating where star performers are located in your organization, you may uncover "clusters" of star performers (for example, in a particular geography, region, or division). Typically, these clusters of star performers lead you to consider whether exemplary managers are the true stars. Whether you ultimately identify an individual, team, or exemplary manager as the principal driver behind success, your search should begin with the identification of what the organization considers the relevant performance metrics or KPIs. To be clear, the performance data we are referring to is around the business metrics that matter to the organization; we are not referring to performance appraisals.

For example, in our work with an insurance industry client, we first determined that net profit from premiums was a key metric for the company. When we met with the star performers who delivered the highest results based on this metric, we discovered other critical measures that were being leveraged by the stars, but not being used by typical performers. The star underwriters analyzed their own work by breaking down their premiums by sales channel and then identified in which channel(s) they were underperforming. This became the fertile ground for growing the book of business the following year. There's an important lesson in this: initially, we identified the star performers based on the macro metrics of total net profit from premiums. A common task identified across those star performers was this internal analysis of sales channels. What was learned was then transferable across the workforce of underwriters and produced tremendous value for the organization.

In another client's sales function, the top performers focused on two of five sales channels. Their mental models were not to go after the lower-performing sales channels or try to get equal results across all five. They recognized greater profitability (greater margins) in two sales channels and that's where they placed most of their focus. The average salespeople in this organization had more of a balanced approach to the sales channels. The vital point here is that identifying accomplishments and metrics depends heavily on a specific organizational context. So rather than capture the mental models of the entire sales staff and then replicate the most common or most popular sales models across the sales force (thereby perpetuating average performance!), we captured the models of the star performers based on the most relevant client data and shared their strategy across the entire sales force.

If we examine data from a national chain of retail auto parts stores, we can see the potential error of just accepting readily available data. Table 3.1 shows annual revenues at individual stores:

Table 3.1. Annual Revenue for Auto Parts Stores

Store	Revenue (in $M)
A	3.2
B	3.8
C	2.6
D	2.2
E	3.7
. . .	. . .

Looking at one year's revenue figures tells only part of the story and would not be a sufficient way to identify high-performing store managers. The following are items that need to be considered in this example:

- Look at year over year revenue, not just a single year.
- Normalize the data for store size (X square feet versus Y square feet).
- Account for local variables such as demographics, competition, and so on. How would you rate store performance if you found that Store E has produced $3.7 million in revenue when the rival competition has a store directly across the street, whereas Store B has no significant competition within four miles?

We would also ask the district manager what other measures are relevant in selecting high-performing store managers to replicate. We might hear profitability, control of costs, employee turnover, and so forth. One major retailer we know has an expected annual loss due to theft (primarily internal) of $2 billion annually. You can imagine that a store manager that successfully controls this type of loss would be a good candidate for cloning!

Determining How Many Exemplars to Observe/Interview

First, exemplary performers, by definition, are few in number compared to the number of "typical" performers. Second, our experience on determining the study size allows us to make the following observations and comments:

- The greater the variance among individuals or teams, the greater the return on investment for the project.
- Performance variance increases as job complexity increases.

To illustrate the return on investment observation, we have found as much as a 200% to 300% difference in the sales performance of some stars and the average performance of their colleagues. Still, the fact remains that the size of the sample you choose to observe and interview depends on some experience-based statistics.

For example, an organization with an 800-person sales team will have only 18 performers who fall more than two standard deviations above the average (see Figure 3.1). This fact does help determine the number we will want to observe or interview. Project constraints are always a key factor. For example, a limited travel budget can have a significant impact, as we attempt to interview at least half of these high performers in face-to-face interaction. The rest of the potential exemplars might require only a phone interview or an exchange of substantive e-mails, as you validate your findings and draw conclusions from the time spent directly observing and interviewing the first half of the exemplary performers.

The same statistical metric applies, even with a smaller pool of potential high performers. For an initial pool of 400 individuals

Figure 3.1. Bell Curve or Normal Distribution

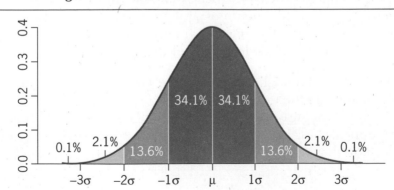

in a sales role, you'd find nine performers who are two standard deviations above the mean. In this case, interviewing and observing all nine is both possible and advisable.

If you are thinking that perhaps the time and expense of following this process might be reduced by just observing a single top performer and then basing all your recommendations on this single case, think again! Our experience has shown us over and over that the exemplar (the single best performer) is not always the highest performer across *all* outputs for that particular role. Typically, different exemplars are best at producing particular outputs and the final role profile is a compilation of the input from all the stars with whom we worked.

Returning to the underwriting example provided earlier, our investigation revealed several major accomplishments for this role. Of the exemplary performers we interviewed, those who were the absolute best at producing "an executable business plan" for their unit fell short of exemplary performance in another output—innovative products and services. However, by interviewing the top eight to ten performers, it was possible to compile a profile that represented best practices across the entire role and would provide the data from which transferable practices could be derived.

Representative Biased Sample Output

If you took a representative sample of the workforce in an organization, it would represent (by definition) the average performance of the typical person or team in a role. It would also produce a description of a job in its current state.

A biased sample—one that intentionally seeks the exemplars from the right side of the bell curve—would:

- Produce a model of performance based on the best performers in the role
- Simultaneously provide best practices or current best approaches, because top performers typically do things more logically and systematically than others

Selecting Your Exemplary Performers

As noted earlier in this chapter, the first step in the process of examining outputs that provide value to an organization is to determine relevant performance metrics. You should be very deliberate in selecting the information to use in selecting exemplary performers.

Identifying exemplary performers through a review of performance appraisals is not an advisable approach.

For example, identifying exemplary performers through a review of performance appraisals is not an advisable approach. In one project in the oil refining industry, the best performer had one of the lowest overall performance appraisal ratings among his peers (along with a thick personnel file full of supporting documentation of his poor performance). His managers—and even his peers—made it clear that this worker was *the* most highly regarded in terms of his on-time performance, safety, and quality accomplishments. The thick personnel file simply reflected the worker's outspoken personality.

Quantitative and Qualitative Measures—Case Study

To further demonstrate the point illustrated above, here is another example. The senior VP of operations of this Fortune 500 company considered two key metrics—gross revenue and cost—as most important for the geographically dispersed business leaders who were the focus of this study. The senior VP further weighted these metrics by saying that gross revenue was twice as important as operating cost. He further refined his expectations for these two metrics by adjusting the specific expected results to take into account local business unit market maturity, the competition in that market, and state regulations.

Based on this information, we worked with a variety of stakeholders to produce two spreadsheets based on measures that were already in use by the organization. The five measures are presented in Table 3.2.

In discussing these metrics with the senior VP of operations, we found, not unexpectedly, that some metrics were of greater

Table 3.2. Metrics for Identifying Exemplary Business Unit Leaders

Measure	Explanation
Revenue Growth	Percentage of revenue growth year over year
Margin	Percentage increase in operating margin (gross profit) year over year
Employee Satisfaction	Single metric from employee satisfaction survey
Customer Satisfaction: Category A Category B	Single metric (0–100) from customer surveys, segmented into two customer categories
Quality Indicator	Rolled up quality metric (Note: In this particular industry, quality is more important than price or speed.)

importance than others. When discussing the individual business leader results (see Table 3.3 on the next page), the refinement resulted in the following guidance:

- Choose the top three performers based primarily on revenue growth and margin.
- Don't include anyone with employee satisfaction below 65%, nor quality indices below 85%.

If you look at Table 3.3, you can see that the criteria clearly led to the selection of Pittsburgh, Kansas City, and New York. The work of pulling the data together and talking through priorities with the senior VP gave us what we needed to identify exemplary performers and it also aided the VP in establishing or refining organizational priorities.

Identifying Exemplary Performers in a Government Setting

Routine business metrics are not generally useful for identifying exemplary performers in the military or in federal or state governments. However, the key focus is still on the accomplishments

Table 3.3. Metrics for Business Unit Leaders

Measure:	Pittsburgh	Orlando	Kansas City	New York	Los Angeles
Revenue Growth	15%	8%	6%	11%	2%
Margin	43%	16%	34%	22%	9%
Employee Satisfaction	77%	58%	72%	83%	68%
Customer Satisfaction Category A	84%	78%	78%	81%	73%
Customer Satisfaction Category B	89%	76%	74%	79%	71%
Quality Indices	97%	92%	91%	94%	82%

people produce that provide value to the organization. For example:

- For a government program manager who writes regulations, one accomplishment might be: "new regulation in place with stakeholder buy-in." The criteria might involve a number of quality measures:
  - Effectiveness of new regulations
  - Customer satisfaction (for example, stakeholder alignment)
  - Timeliness in implementing regulation
- For a government contracting officer, the output might be: "contract awarded to capable provider." The criteria might involve:
  - Award made within government cost estimate/budget
  - Customer satisfaction (for example, sponsoring department, potential bidders)
  - Small business goals met
  - Quality of service provided by contractor
  - Accuracy of performance work statement

- For a law enforcement official, one output might be: "admissible evidence packages." The criteria might involve:
  - Witness statements made after proper Mirandizing
  - Chain of custody maintained
  - Search warrants obtained following probable cause

In a government or public setting, identifying exemplary performers based on who has consistently produced accomplishments and associated criteria at a high level can be a challenge. The information is not always measurable or readily obtained. Sometimes "triangulation" from multiple vantage points is necessary to arrive at a satisfactory result. Here are some examples from our practice that illustrate this approach:

- In a federal government setting, we inquired across stakeholder groups about who was judged to be the best at drafting government regulations and then found the same performers identified by multiple stakeholders.
- In a law enforcement setting, we queried assistant U.S. attorneys about those officers who produced case packages that could consistently go forward and those officers whose case packages did not meet standard.
- In the U.S. Navy and Coast Guard, weapons petty officers are responsible for maintaining weapons and ammunition at a unit level, where a unit is defined as a station, cutter, or ship. In the U.S. Coast Guard specifically, smaller units have weapons petty officers (WPO) who perform these duties on a part-time or collateral duty basis, and their occupational specialty (or rating) is not weapons related. Four hundred people in the U.S. Coast Guard currently split their time between this and other assigned duties. Most of the duties for WPO are described in an 800-page servicewide policy manual called the *Ordnance Manual*. There is a checklist in the manual that is used to conduct an annual inspection by each WPO. This manual and checklist can legitimately be viewed as the organizationally approved criteria for job performance.

  Some of the checklist criteria border on being trivial. Other aspects cut right to the heart of value to the organization. For example, "Are weapons maintained, clean, and operationally ready?'' We used this checklist as the basis for conversations with stakeholders in order to discover which items they would use to distinguish good from great performers.

In navigation, when two lines of bearing cross, you have a pretty good idea of your location. Adding a third line of bearing adds significant confidence (instinctively and mathematically). Identifying exemplary performers is analogous. The results of annual inspections is one "line of bearing" to generate a list of potential WPO exemplary performers. Refining and prioritizing items on the annual checklist according to organizational value provided us with greater confidence and, importantly, it shortened the list of possible exemplary performers.

Next we applied a filter of reputation by querying the inspectors who travel to every unit to inspect and maintain quality and consistency. We asked the inspectors to identify who they thought did the best job producing the accomplishments we had identified for the role. This yielded a final list of six exemplary performers the organization was eager to replicate.

Creating "Synthetic" Exemplary Performers

A "synthetic" exemplar is a term we use to describe a situation in which there is no pool of performers to question or observe, such as when there is a newly created job or job category. Sometimes important aspects of a particular job are performed only in emergencies or performed so infrequently that most of the performer group has no experience. In these cases, you must synthesize that missing part of the job performance from other sources.

In order to accomplish this bit of magic, you may need to ask other exemplary performers to speculate how they would perform these tasks, taking care to provide them with any additional information to allow these *stand-in* high performers to imagine how they would perform optimally in that role. In the case of the weapons petty officers, we discovered that one critical aspect of the job was the "Initial response to a weapons-related MISHAP." Not surprisingly, none of our exemplary performers had ever experienced this particular scenario. However, an organizational need certainly existed to provide clear direction (policy, procedures) and performance support (such as training, job aids) for all weapons petty officers, should a "weapons-related MISHAP" occur at their unit.

For the parts of jobs which have "high consequences for error" and are performed infrequently or unpredictably, organizations should (and typically do) spend time thinking through and clarifying how people should respond in such circumstances. For instance, you don't want your pilot to be the most experienced at crashing planes. We want a pilot to have demonstrated great proficiency in a simulator across a spectrum of in-flight emergencies. The procedures used in the simulator (and in a real-life emergency) should be the product of design engineers—in addition to experienced pilots, instructor pilots, and subject-matter experts who have studied relevant factors in previous in-flight emergencies—who can explain how a plane and its equipment react under certain conditions.

Validation of Exemplary Performer Selection

Eventually, all the work you put into exemplary performer selection comes down to a single question—whose performance *do* you want to replicate? Clearly, the answer should be those individuals who consistently produce valued outputs at or above standard. Here is a summary of how to produce your list of exemplars.

First, don't rely on gut instinct alone or on measures unrelated to outputs of value. Next, remember that a draft list of exemplary performers is produced in a variety of ways. Sometimes you have to take a quantitative approach, and at other times you may have to take a more qualitative route to determine the true high performers. In some cases, finding high performers might require a mix of both approaches. Third, remember the context. We may start with existing organizational data or the manager may already have a list of candidates. If a manager already has a list, we should ensure that additional data is reviewed to either confirm the candidates or to serve as the basis for challenging the selections. The data should be understood in the context of the organization being studied. If you recall the case study that involved the senior VP of operations at one of our client companies, you'll remember that exemplary performer validation greatly improved when the metrics we used to select exemplary performers were adjusted to align with the true organizational and strategic goals. In our case study, the VP of operations told us that revenue was the first priority and that controlling costs was the second priority. However, the caveat to those performance parameters was to not include any business unit manager with poor employee satisfaction scores. In this case, employee satisfaction was not the key driver, yet it was still a factor in selecting exemplary performers.

In the oil industry example, the fact that the exemplary performer was outspoken was not as important as the safety, innovation, and process improvement results the individual had demonstrated. In the Coast Guard example, the formal assessment was a factor, but not the deciding factor. Instead, it was only through "triangulation" of prioritized items on a checklist and additional insights from inspectors and supervisors that we were able to identify the exemplars.

Summary

This chapter provided you with several methods for identifying your internal star performers. Once selected for a particular project, the next step is to create a rich model of their performance. The next chapter provides a description of this process for capturing the Profile of Exemplary Performance.

CHAPTER FOUR

Capturing the Expertise
of Your Stars

In This Chapter

- An Accomplishment-Based Approach to
  Capturing Expertise
- Creating a Profile of Exemplary Performance
- A Case Study

By this point, we're sure that you agree with our position that it's results (accomplishments) that matter more than just the raw talent or potential of your team. And as a quick review, you have probably begun to think about how to:

- Identify the functions or roles that are most critical to executing your strategy and achieving your goals
- Prioritize the opportunities for shifting the performance curve
- Compare the accomplishments of your team's stars with solid, but average performers
- Select your accomplished performers (your stars) and list the most critical business metrics tied to high-priority opportunities

This chapter provides an overview of our approach for capturing the expertise of exemplary performers by using a "right to

Figure 4.1. Analyzing Right to Left

Influences	Behavior	Accomplishments	Goals
Skills/ knowledge	Sell products	Revenues	Profits
Motivation	Make decisions	Plans	High returns
Supportive environment	Diagnose problems	Delighted customers	Customer satisfaction

Performance **unfolds** in this direction ⟶

⟵ We **analyze** in this direction

Source: Exemplary Performance, LLC.

left'' analysis approach discussed briefly in Chapter One. As you recall, this approach enables you to move from strategy and goals to critical accomplishments; from accomplishments to the key activities and decisions that produce those accomplishments; and from those key behaviors to the identification of the requisite support required across the six components of a high-performance work system—the Exemplary Performance System. Figure 4.1 will help you establish the logic of this approach as you work through this chapter.

An Accomplishment-Based Approach to Capturing Expertise

Remember, your exemplary performers are often unconsciously competent!

The most effective and efficient way to capture expertise is to work with your existing accomplished performers— your internal benchmarks. These are the individuals who have established approaches to their work that produce the desired accomplishments at a consistently high level. As you recall from our earlier discussion, these exemplary performers are often unconsciously competent, and thus you will need to capture their expertise in a way to make it explicit and transferable to other team members.

The process presented in this chapter is a tested approach for capturing exemplars' hidden expertise based on our work with hundreds of clients across multiple industries.[1] Our experience has shown us that asking stars why they are good at what they do or how they go about doing their work just leads to meaningless banter about their education, work history, intelligence, competencies, and other variables that have little or nothing to do with how these individuals produce exceptional results.

Instead, the analysis of accomplished performers must be context-intensive and case-based. For example, if you're working with a sales team that consistently wins competitive displacements, it's best to ask them to walk you through several recent wins in a detailed and methodical way. The questioning should address every step in the process, from the identification of the opportunity, to closing the sale, to full implementation of the product or service. Your investigation would include at least the following questions to the team or individual performer(s):

Capturing the true accomplishment is often the most critical aspect of the process.

- What did you consider when determining your approach to the opportunity?
- Was the sales team already in place or was it formed specifically for this opportunity?
- If it was formed to address this specific opportunity, what factors did you consider when selecting sales team members?
- What were the critical steps in the sales process, and where did key handoffs occur?[2]

Here's an example of this process based on recent work with a client that requested a detailed analysis of several high-performing global sales teams. The teams selected for analysis were winning sales opportunities against a key competitor at a much higher percentage than other sales teams in the company.

We began the process with one team in a meeting that lasted several hours, during which the team identified the most critical aspects of the entire sales cycle for the particular win. The discussion revealed that both the sales team and their customer agreed that the proof of concept (POC)—developed by the technical sales specialist on the team—was one of the key differentiators that led the customer to select our client's solution.

We set up a meeting with Monique, the highly praised technical sales specialist on the team, and asked to meet in her office the next day. This would provide us with access to the critical POC documentation. We asked her to walk us through the process she used to produce what we thought was the critical output—the POC. In the course of the conversation, Monique had an "aha" moment. She suddenly realized that her accomplishment was not the POC itself. Rather, Monique realized that her approach to creating POCs was what made her a star performer. Her true accomplishment was how she leveraged the POC to create an internal advocate for adopting her solution inside the client company.

Monique's insight was that, instead of building the POC by herself, she scripted it based on thorough knowledge of the competitor's existing tool. She identified the client's current pain points with the tool they were using and then designed a solution based on her company's product. Once the problem was identified, Monique contacted a person of high influence inside the customer organization and scheduled a meeting. When they met, she and the client built a customized POC together, based on the script she had already created. Not only was the client impressed, but Monique's proactive approach created an advocate inside the client's organization for her proposed solution. That advocate was then willing to spend two weeks convincing his colleagues to go with Monique's proposed solution.

Once we understood Monique's true accomplishment—an internal customer advocate—we built a tool that other technical sales specialists could use to replicate Monique's approach to leveraging POCs within client organizations in order to establish internal advocacy. Our tool was used to rapidly deploy and apply Monique's approach across multiple ongoing competitive sales opportunities.

One thing that differentiates accomplished performers from solid performers is their use of rich mental models.

We find that this kind of "aha" experience happens with some frequency during the performance analysis process. Like Monique, exemplars go about doing their work without ever taking the time to clearly define what leads to their own success. Stars make the assumption that their colleagues approach their work using the same rich mental models that they have developed based on codifying years and years of experience; it is these rich models that differentiate the accomplished performers from the merely solid performers. By capturing these models (a key element of the star's profile), you can shorten the "time to competence" for the other members of the team.

Creating a Profile of Exemplary Performance

Capturing the expertise of high performers in your organization provides a rich repository of information that describes optimal work performance. We call this the Profile of Exemplary Performance (PEP). The information in the PEP is useful to design and implement a wide range of performance interventions, from hiring to compensation, training to assessment, and process improvements to recognition and reward systems. You can think of the PEP as the DNA of your exemplars.

Leveraging the Profile of Exemplary Performance allows you to shift the performance curve optimally to the right, getting the maximum results from your existing resources.

The PEP data includes such information as the accomplishments produced by the particular role or team, the success criteria for those accomplishments, the key activities, tasks, and decisions that produce the accomplishments, and system facilitators and barriers that the stars have discovered. You can then use this unique data set, the PEP, as the design basis for building a *performance architecture*—an integrated set of solutions designed to maximize the performance of everyone in the targeted role or team. This performance architecture, which carefully aligns all six subsystems that comprise the EPS, will optimize the shift of the performance curve.

Figure 4.2 shows the desired result of using the PEP as the *common design basis* for all components of the performance systems. The six system components are aligned and integrated, producing exemplary performance for the targeted role or roles, enabling you to get maximum results from your existing resources.

Use of the PEP has significant economic implications for your organization, because *greater results produced by your existing workforce ultimately have a direct impact on the bottom line.* How do you start? Here's the process.

Business Analysis and Alignment — An Essential Step

Before you begin any analysis, you must first align the purpose of the project with the organization's business strategy and

Figure 4.2. Aligning Performance System Components

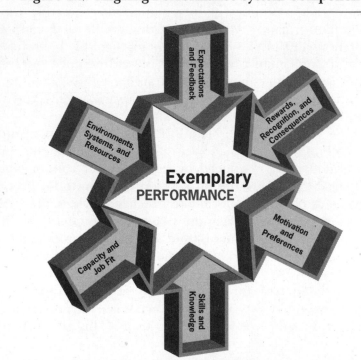

Source: Exemplary Performance, LLC. Copyright 2008–2012.

goals. Remember, you do this analysis from right to left! (See Figure 4.1.) Thus, a formal alignment meeting, which includes the client, is essential. The outcome of the meeting is to verify and clarify the situation that led to the request for the analysis. Make sure that you invite all key stakeholders, along with members of the analysis team.

Our experience indicates that initial consensus is rare between the client and other stakeholders regarding the project's purpose, the business goal it supports, and how project success should be measured. For example, is the goal of the analysis to improve customer satisfaction or enhance profits? Make sure you establish alignment across the key stakeholders *prior* to beginning the analysis, not just between the project team and the client.

Next, you need to capture indicators of success that are operational and, preferably, quantitative:

- How do the client and the stakeholders visualize and assess organizational performance on a day-to-day basis?
- What are the parameters and constraints of the project?
- When does the client require the results?
- Who are the exemplary performers?
- Where are they located? How many sites need to be visited?
- Are there any budget and travel constraints?

It's also essential to determine roles *within* the project and to identify who will be the final authority on determining the accuracy of the results and usefulness of the recommendations.

Another important component of the business analysis phase is the clarification and validation of the organization's goals. This is essential for two reasons. First, these goals determine how the results of the analysis are evaluated. Ultimately, the client wants any data and recommendations coming out of the analysis to directly affect the achievement of those goals. Second, workers perform best when they know what their company is trying to accomplish and how their individual results fit into the big picture—"the worth of their work." Remember that goals, even if they are clearly stated, must also be clearly communicated to workers. Unfortunately, many workers don't understand the relationship between their work and their company's goals, and this significantly inhibits optimal performance. Following is an extreme example.

A colleague of mine happened to be visiting a manufacturing facility on the same day that a 30-year employee was retiring. During the retirement ceremony, the employee's managers asked how he would like to spend his last day on the job. Surprisingly, the employee said that he would like to be given a tour of the entire plant. You see, he had never seen the entire facility and just wanted to understand how his job fit together with the entire operation. Though this true story may be an extreme case, we encounter this type of scenario all the time. It is hard (perhaps impossible) to be a superstar if you don't understand the worth of your work.

Stars as Internal Benchmarks

Benchmarking the best practices of other companies is a common practice, but many organizations run into difficulty implementing these new approaches back into their own organizations. The stumbling blocks might be differences in corporate cultures or a whole host of other reasons. One advantage to creating PEPs is that this process captures best practices (or benchmarks) from within the same organizational culture, thus avoiding this problem. Another advantage is that the PEP process allows for much more rapid implementation. Now let's take a closer look at the process for creating PEPs.

From the Field, For the Field

Here are the critical steps involved in conducting a performance analysis:

- Determine the key accomplishments that exemplary performers produce.
- Collect data on those accomplishments.
- Produce a task list for each accomplishment.
- Collect key data on each of the tasks.

In an ideal environment, it's best to collect data on accomplishments and tasks by interviewing and observing exemplary performers. Don't rely on a task force or focus group for reliable and valid information, because the characteristics or behaviors that differentiate the exemplar from the average performer are often subtle and intuitive. These nuances will not be self-reported through an interview process alone. The process requires observation, combined with debriefing after the performance, to "get inside the skin" of the star. If actual observation is not possible or practical, case-based interviews are a good alternative. Case-based analysis works well if you are able to walk the star or team through real cases, while they answer questions based on actual data and project documents that can be accessed during the analysis process.

Of course, exemplary performers may not be available due to atypical circumstances, such as new technologies that have not yet been deployed, new processes yet to be launched, or new roles that need to be designed. In the case of new technology or processes, you might work with the technology provider to find noncompetitive organizations that have already implemented the technology or process.

When performance analysis is required to create or support a new job, you might benchmark some of the accomplishments of the new job against similar accomplishments in existing positions. Or you might spend time with exemplary performers who are currently performing parts of the new job. Often the analysis for a new job will be a composite based on multiple current stars who are performing portions of the new role—or at least are doing work that is analogous to the new role.

Of course, there are occasions when you don't have access to *any* exemplary performer, either inside or outside your organization. In these cases, you'll have to rely on other data sources such as a task force of people currently performing similar work. You might also try interviewing the process or technology designer to gather needed data for your analysis. Please note that none of these alternative data sources provide the quality of data you'll get from a superstar who has developed deep expertise by codifying years, if not decades, of experience.

Determine the Key Accomplishments

So where do you begin to create your PEP? First, develop a summary statement that captures the overall purpose of the job. You can begin by asking questions such as: "What is the overall accomplishment, result, or output of this job?" or "What is the main thing you produce that contributes to the success of your team or organization?"

Once you have developed a draft of the job accomplishment, you then create a list of the key accomplishments that are routinely produced by people in this role. Questions here might include an inquiry as simple as, "What do you produce during a routine day, week, or month?" This question leads to follow-on questions, such as accomplishments produced on a nonroutine basis. Note that in many cases these nonroutine accomplishments carry a high consequence of error, so pay attention. Table 4.1 shows the job summary and major accomplishments for a project manager.

Table 4.1. Project Manager Job Summary and Major Accomplishments

Job Summary	Projects delivered within budget or at above projected gross profit
Routine Accomplishments	Project plans Deliverables produced on time and to standard
Nonroutine Accomplishments	Troubleshooting client complaints to produce maximum client satisfaction and minimum negative effect on project profitability and company reputation

Collect Data on Accomplishments

With the specific accomplishments identified for the job, now you are ready to collect data on each accomplishment. First, identify the criteria or standards for each accomplishment. Have the exemplary performer answer this question: "How do you determine a good accomplishment from an inferior one?"

In most cases, these criteria fall under the categories of accuracy, time, productivity, or safety. Next, look for any anticipated changes that might affect the accomplishment in the near future, such as reorganizations, new equipment or technology, or changes in policy, regulations, or procedures.

Then determine how much time the star spends producing this particular accomplishment in a typical week or month. Table 4.2 is an example of data collected on one major accomplishment of a project manager.

Table 4.2. Data Collected on Project Plan

Major Accomplishment	Project plan
Percentage of Project Time	5%
Major Criteria	Plan clearly describes scope of work, deliverables, work breakdown, resources, schedule, cost, assumptions
Anticipated Changes	No changes likely in overall approach to project planning; however, each project requires specific tailoring of planning steps
Interactions	Project director, project staff, customer, stakeholders, peers who may be involved with similar projects

Produce a Task List for Each Accomplishment

The next step in the process is the creation of a task list for each accomplishment. For the record, a task is a unit of behavior with a clear beginning, and it includes a process composed of two or more steps that contribute to a desired output. For example, if you called AAA to fix a flat tire, the desired accomplishment might be a "vehicle that is safe and ready to drive." When the tow truck shows up, the driver would need to perform several tasks: jack the car, loosen the wheel, remove the wheel, replace the wheel, and lower the car. Each of the tasks has a clear beginning, a series of steps, and a result. For example, the result of jacking up the car is weight off the wheel. However, as a customer, you will not pay for the wheel being removed in isolation from the desired accomplishment, which is a car ready to drive. Another way of thinking about this is that tasks produce outputs, but accomplishments produce value. As the task list is the basis for almost all subsequent analysis work, you should take the time to be rigorous.

Sometimes, an exemplary performer will have a *draft* task list. If that's the case, make sure the list is accurate and still relevant. Ask the star whether any of the tasks are part of another job or another accomplishment. Check to ensure that no tasks are missing and review the wording of each task to make sure the terminology is accurate.

If a task list is not available, observing the exemplary performer doing the actual work and generating a task list in real time will give you the best results. However, if the task takes too long for you to actually observe, ask the exemplary performer to simulate the process of producing the accomplishment while you observe. Table 4.3 is an abbreviated task list for producing a project plan.

Tasks produce outputs, but accomplishments produce value.

This real-time analysis process works effectively, even if the work is cognitive in nature. For example, suppose you need to analyze the process of a loan officer reaching a decision about whether or not to grant a loan to an applicant. You would likely observe how an application is reviewed, how policy and procedure manuals are accessed, and perhaps even

Table 4.3. Task List

Major Accomplishment	Project Plan
Tasks	Prepare work breakdown structure
	Complete project pricing proposal
	Write proposal
	Negotiate proposal and obtain purchase order
	Set up project baseline
	Write detailed project plan

interactions with colleagues. (Note: This case analysis is optimally done in the real work environment.)

At the end of the analysis, perform an extensive debriefing, using the notes you made. Your exchange might sound something like this:

"When reviewing the application, what are the key things you look for?"

"I review the application to determine the creditworthiness of the applicant."

"What data do you use to determine whether the applicant is creditworthy?" and so forth.

Collect Key Data on the Tasks

To determine the criteria for each task you identify, you might ask the star performer questions such as:

"How do you know when the task is complete?"

"How would you judge that the task has been done correctly?"

Examine any available documentation with the exemplary performer in order to capture critical data on each task you have analyzed. You will use this set of data to make important decisions when you design interventions. Task characteristics to focus on include:

- *Speed*: Is speed a factor in performing the task. Do seconds count?
- *Task environment*: Are there any characteristics of the environment that are particularly noteworthy? For example, would it be difficult for a worker to use a job aid or performance support?
- *Frequency*: How often is the task done?
- *Complexity*: How many steps are in the task, and are any steps particularly difficult?
- *Task change*: What is the probability that the task will change in any significant way within the foreseeable future?
- *Consequences of error*: If the task is performed incorrectly or below standard, could the deficient performance result in loss of life, injury, or economic damage?

Your work thus far has generated a significant amount of data; thus, it's a good idea to validate your work before continuing. You might have your data reviewed by stars in other parts of the organization or engage technical experts or others in the organization familiar with policies, procedures, and safety regulations. However, the ultimate validation is provided by the client and key stakeholders. (See the Appendix for sample data for one major accomplishment and the tasks required to produce that accomplishment for a technical sales role.)

Performance Analysis — A Continuous Improvement Tool

At some time you may want to support an improvement initiative rather than analyzing an entire role or process. To leverage performance analysis in this way, you would identify the problems, the reasons why the problems exist, and how to resolve them. Here are the steps you would take to do this type of analysis:

1. Identify the deficient output(s) or accomplishment(s) that triggered the issue.
2. Define the tasks of the deficient accomplishment.
3. Determine where inadequate human performance is causing the deficient accomplishment.
4. Generate cause hypotheses.
5. Identify probable causes and make recommendations.

Be sure to identify any current measurements that are tied to the deficient accomplishment. Review the data on historic performance and compare it to expected performance. If hard data is not available, explore what anecdotal data is available and would be acceptable to the client. It is essential that you achieve consensus with the stakeholders at the beginning of the project on what needs to be measured, which data will be acceptable, and how your efforts in analysis and potential intervention design will be assessed in relationship to any improvements. The results you provide at the end of the analysis will only be credible to the client if you have achieved consensus on how to measure those results from the beginning.

Often the request to analyze a deficit will come from the client, along with a specific solution that the client had in mind. For example, the client requests training on some topic instead of asking for help in improving performance. The recommended response to a solution request is to state, "Yes, I can help you with that. Can you tell me more about the situation that led you to this request?" With most requests for specific solutions, try to identify what is not being achieved in the client's organization. To obtain answers to this question, you might ask questions like these:

"If this project were successful, what would change in your organization?"

"Is there some current goal or result for which your team is
responsible that is currently being produced below standard?"

Be sure that you have clearly defined the gap between current performance and desired performance, tying it directly to business goals. If at all possible, determine the potential financial value of resolving the problem.

Once you have identified the deficient major accomplishment, obtain or generate a task list. As discussed earlier, have the exemplary performer produce or simulate the production of the major accomplishment, while you observe to validate the task list. Distinguish between those tasks that are being performed adequately and those that are being performed below standard. You can determine this by reviewing existing data, observing exemplary performers, and comparing your findings with observations of average performance. Interviewing incumbents, managers, and technical experts also are useful methods. Look for the following:

- Tasks that are not being performed at all;
- Tasks that are not being performed fast enough;
- Tasks in which errors are made in some of the steps;
- Tasks that are not being performed safely;
- Tasks in which steps are performed out of order;
- Tasks in which steps have been added that are not required; and
- Tasks that require a lot of coaching.

You might also try to ascertain whether the deficient performance occurs at a particular time or place.

Once you've identified the deficient tasks, you can generate a cause hypothesis, addressing why the tasks are not performed adequately. Begin by clustering possible hypotheses into the six categories of the Exemplary Performance System. The following are examples for three of the categories:

- For the Skills/Knowledge category, consider whether workers know how to perform the task, when to perform the task, and whether or not they are familiar with the standards for the task.
- For the Environmental category, examine work conditions as well as the type of equipment and tools workers use.
- For the Rewards, Recognition, and Consequences category, consider whether workers are rewarded for performing the task correctly and if there are consequences for performing below standard.

Now it's time to capture data to identify probable causes for the deficiencies and make general recommendations to your client. Hold a meeting with the client and the stakeholders who participated in the alignment process. Make sure you let the participants know that the meeting is to validate and verify the information, not to simply present your results for acceptance or rejection.

Here is an example to illustrate the process: The maintenance managers at a large company were exceeding their budgets by 7% to 23%. A performance analyst took on the challenge of analyzing the issue. The analysis revealed that managers prepared their budgets without input and support. Many of the managers did not know how to estimate costs accurately or how to justify their numbers to superiors. In addition, the analysis found that managers were given feedback only twice a year on how much money they spent. Strangely enough, managers who overspent their budgets were even being "rewarded" by having their maintenance monies increased the following year.

The performance analyst for this project recommended several interventions, including training for maintenance managers on projecting maintenance costs, preparing budgets based on those costs, and justifying budgets. The managers were also provided technical assistance from the financial department during budget preparation. Monthly reports were adjusted to show actual versus projected spending on each line item, significantly reducing the delay in feedback on their performance. Finally, the company established a policy that overspending would have a negative impact on a manager's performance evaluation.

Evaluating the Success of Your Analysis

Rigorous performance analysis is the tool of choice whenever you want to shift the performance curve optimally to the right. It allows you to produce greater results with existing resources by replicating the results of your exemplary performers. The success of your analysis depends on whether the major accomplishments of the job meet the organization's standards of quantity, quality, and cost. If, at the end of the project, the accomplishments still don't meet those standards, you should assess which interventions were inadequate and make improvements as necessary.

A Case Study

The following case study illustrates how performance analysis can significantly accelerate the launch of new technology, new work processes, or a new organizational design. A refinery decided to enter the asphalt market, so it began by conducting a detailed performance analysis. The goal was to load and dispatch an asphalt delivery truck safely in less than 30 minutes from the time it arrived at the refinery's gate.

To ensure a successful market entry, a performance analyst worked with management to identify company goals based on the needs of potential customers. The analyst then studied every facet of human performance that would be involved, including blending, testing, certifying, loading, and handling paperwork. He also identified the major accomplishments and tasks required to meet the goal of dispatching the truck safely within 30 minutes. Finally, the analyst translated these accomplishments and tasks into work procedures, training, and job aids to ensure high performance for all workers involved in the process—from the operators blending the asphalt to the security force controlling truck traffic.

As a result of the work, the asphalt facility showed a 75% return-on-investment in the first year of operation, and part of this success was attributed to the targeted analysis that had been performed and the interventions derived from it.

Summary

This chapter has provided a field-tested approach for capturing the *profile* of your stars. These exemplary performers are the individuals who have established approaches to their work that consistently produce the desired accomplishments at an optimal level. You can think of these exemplars as internal benchmarks who are operating within the same organizational structure and culture as the rest of your employees; yet, these individuals have found ways to exceed the organization's expectations.

The data you capture from your stars will lead to the creation of a Profile of Exemplary Performance (PEP). As you will see in Part Two of this book, the PEP can then serve as the foundation for a performance architecture that aligns all the support required across the six components of a high-performance work system. This will allow you to shift the performance curve optimally to the right, producing significant improvements for your team and the enterprise it supports.

The next chapter answers a question that we are asked more frequently than any other: "Are there common traits of exemplary performers regardless of role or function?" Let's see what makes them tick!

Notes

1. P. H. Elliott, "Assessment," in *Moving from Training to Performance*, eds. D. G. & J. C. Robinson (San Francisco: ASTD & Berrett-Koehler, 1998).
2. P. H. Elliott, "Identifying Learning and Performance Gaps," in *ASTD Handbook for Workplace Learning Professionals*, ed. E. Biech (Alexandria, VA: ASTD, 2008).

CHAPTER FIVE

What Makes Them Tick?

How Stars and Exemplary Teams Consistently
Exceed Expectations

In This Chapter

- A Poignant Example: "Brace for Impact!"
- The Myths of What Makes Stars
- What Makes Them Tick?
- The Exemplary Performance System (EPS) Model

A Poignant Example: "Brace for Impact!"

These were the terrifying words Captain Chesley "Sully" Sullenberger, delivered to the 150 passengers aboard the Airbus A320 on January 15, 2009, only minutes after taking off from New York's LaGuardia Airport. The seasoned pilot of the now famous USAIR flight 1549 had just lifted off for a routine flight to Charlotte, North Carolina, when the plane struck a flock of geese flying directly through its flight path. Improbably, the collision with the geese damaged both engines severely. So with one engine on fire and the other one shutting down, he took the only option he had: ditching the plane in the frigid waters of New York Harbor. It took every bit of his 29 years of experience, but Captain Sully performed a textbook water landing in the harbor, saving the lives of all the passengers and crew.

In a subsequent interview with Katie Couric on the CBS News show *60 Minutes*, Captain Sullenberger told the talk show host how he felt when he realized his situation: "It was the worst sickening, pit-of-your-stomach, falling-through-the-floor-feeling I've ever felt in my life."[1]

Clearly, Captain Sullenberger is an extraordinary performer. Imagine if we could replicate Sullenberger's ability in other pilots to handle even the most difficult and stressful circumstances. The case of this high-performing pilot illustrates the two most important lessons we have gleaned from our work with dozens of organizations of all types:

- Variation in results between stars and average performers is *radically underestimated.*
- Organizations do not typically capture and leverage the potential organizational benefits of their exemplary performers.

We have found these two points to be a near constant in our work with organizations, even when the dramatic results of pursuing this strategy of internal benchmarking are so clearly visible. Whether it's performing an emergency landing on water, taking a risky spacewalk to repair the perspective-changing Hubble telescope, or exceeding sales quotas by 100%, we all wonder what these star performers have in common and, whatever it is, can I bottle it for the rest of my team? This chapter provides an overview of these common characteristics, based on our work with many Fortune 100 companies and government agencies, such as the U.S. Coast Guard.

> *Organizations do not typically capture the potential benefits that are available by leveraging exemplary performance.*

The Differences Between Performers

We all readily acknowledge that wide variance exists in how individuals perform in their work settings. Some people are extremely efficient in their work, while others may be regarded as the "go-to" person for the right answers, latest information, or creative solutions.

As we've discussed in previous chapters, the differences between people in terms of the meaningful results they produce is typically underestimated and often attributed to immutable traits such as "raw" talent, intelligence, etc. When the performance gap between an average performer and an exemplary performer is actually measured, the delta is nothing short of startling.

When the performance gap between an average performer and a superstar is actually measured, the delta is nothing short of startling.

Of course, the performance difference among individual workers is not a new observation. In fact, the vast difference between these performers was the central focus of a 1997 study by the consulting firm McKinsey & Company. In their 2001 book based on the study, *The War for Talent*, Michaels, Handfield-Jones, and Axelrod noted the strategic importance of retaining and cultivating these star performers.[2] The authors suggested a talent retention strategy for organizations that emphasized strengthening their talent pool by investing in what the study called A-players, developing second-tier or B-players, and acting decisively on lower-tier C-players.

Even more interesting, as it relates to the topic of this book, is what the five-year study discovered about the bottom-line performance of these A-players compared to B- and C-players. It turns out that those labeled as A-players grew company revenue by 52%, whereas the B-players grew revenue by only 4%. C-players actually shrunk revenue on average by 15% (see Table 5.1). Imagine the impact on the companies studied if the B-players performed more like the A-players! *That's the promise of this book for organizations and their leaders: leveraging the insights and practices of A-players to help B-players achieve exemplary results.*

Table 5.1. Revenue Impact by Worker Group

Worker Group:	A-players	B-players	C-players
Revenue Impact:	52%	4%	−15%

Source: McKinsey & Company, 1997[3]

While we work regularly with a wide variety of businesses and industries across multiple functions, we have found the widest documented performance gap between average and star performers to be in the sales function. According to a 2003 Sales Executive Council study (*Shifting the Performance Curve*),[4] the top 20% of salespeople in organizations consistently outperform the middle 60% of performers combined by an additional 60%. To make sense of this statistic, imagine that an organization employs ten salespeople. If the top two salespeople (20% of the sales force) generated combined sales of $3,000,000 in 2011, then the next six salespeople's combined sales in 2011 would only amount to $1,875,000!

This performance gap also extends to sales teams (prevalent in more complex selling environments) and both the Sales Executive Council and McKinsey studies offered surprising results when teams were examined. McKinsey's study found that top-performing sales teams outperform average sales teams by 180%. In practical terms, this would mean that if the average sales team produced $1,000,000 in sales in a given year, then the top-performing sales team would produce $2,800,000 during that same year. Expressed in context of the bell curve used in this book, this gap translates into the following graphic (Figure 5.1).

Figure 5.1. Sales Team Performance

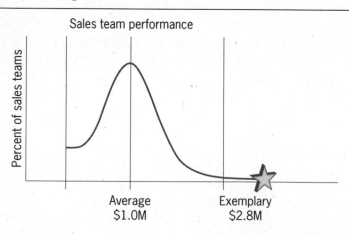

The Myths of What Makes Stars

After working with over one hundred different roles across industries and functions, *we are convinced that any organization can gain a competitive advantage and improve business results by leveraging the strength of their own star performers.* The first four chapters of this book are about the value gained by leveraging the insights of exemplary performers. Part Two is about how to apply what is learned and enabling exceptional results by architecting a system for high performance.

We are repeatedly asked about where superstars come from. What makes them tick? Do they share common characteristics? How did they develop their levels of expertise? The answer is somewhat complex. We begin with some commonly held assumptions (and perhaps even conclusions) about star performers. They include:

> *Just because someone appears to be a natural born leader or salesperson—or naturally smart—does not mean he or she will inevitably become a superstar.*

- Talent
- Competency
- Educational background
- Skills and knowledge
- Motivation
- 10,000 hours of experience

Talent

As Geoff Colvin suggests in his 2008 bestselling book, *Talent Is Overrated: What Really Separates World-Class Performers from Everybody Else,*[5] we agree that talent alone does not make a star performer. Just because someone appears to be a natural born leader or salesperson—or is innately smart—does not mean he or she will inevitably become a superstar. At best, these attributions are correlative, not causative.

Sports provide some easy examples. You might conclude that to be an NFL offensive lineman, the main requirement is weighing 300 pounds or more. But clearly not all persons over 300 pounds are on the list to be an NFL offensive lineman. You might also assume that the "smarts" of a high-tech sales professional translates into star performance on the job. Yet, the reality is that very bright individuals may be average performers (or perhaps even below-average performers) in terms of providing valued results to the company.

Competency

Many organizations use a formalized competency framework to define the general skills that they believe are essential to

Focusing on improving an employee's competencies doesn't correlate with the desired improvements in performance.

building superstars. No doubt many of these models offer standardized competencies that are correlated to what workers need to produce maximum results. Still, our practice has revealed some fundamental limitations using a competency framework.

The following are some observations about the value of competency frameworks. Generally, competency frameworks:

- Do not correlate with desired improvements in performance and are largely viewed as an HR tool. In addition, line managers do not see these competencies as a reliable way to distinguish high performers from average performers. Focusing on improving an employee's competencies doesn't correlate with the desired improvements in performance.
- Do not provide much value for line managers if the competencies are generalized. For instance, some organizations require a "communications" competency for all employees from entry-level administrative staff to top-tier executives. Our experience is that such a generalized competency holds little value for those managers responsible for specific business results.
- Lack the application-specific context across organizational functions and departments. For example, a competency of business acumen in one department may not mean the same thing in another department or at another location serving a different market.
- Do not provide an accurate assessment or description of the valued accomplishments required in a particular role or job, even when great similarities exist between jobs in terms of personality similarities or even defined competencies. Figure 5.2 is

Figure 5.2. What Makes a High Performer?

	A certain personality type	With defined competencies	Who can produce accomplishments
What they are:	A certain personality type	With defined competencies	Who can produce accomplishments
How to define:	• MBTI • Hogan	• McClelland • Hay Group	Accomplishment-based approach
What it shows:	Preferences	Capabilities	Results
EXAMPLE Airline Pilot:	• Attention to detail • Adhere to pattern • Don't experiment	• Choose quickly • Use effective approaches	• Plane safely landed
EXAMPLE Accountant:	• Attention to detail • Adhere to pattern • Don't experiment	• Choose quickly • Use effective approaches	• Tax return properly filed
	If you just focus here		***You don't get this***

Copyright 2011 Greg Long, GP Strategies.

an example of how similar personalities and competencies—in this case between an accountant and a pilot—don't necessarily differentiate between high performance within specific roles.

Educational Background

Educational background, like intelligence, is more of a correlated factor than one of causation. In other words, a better educational background clearly has an impact in certain professions and industries and, in many cases, this necessary *component* for success may not be *sufficient* for success. To say this another way, education may be necessary for many roles, but it is never sufficient to produce superstars. For example, most process engineers in oil refineries have engineering degrees. However, as you might expect, not all are star performers; in fact, most are average. The same dynamic applies to physicians, all of whom have required medical degrees, and yet the number

Education may be necessary for many roles, but it is never sufficient to produce stars.

you might classify as *superstars* is very small. If you'd like to test this assumption, think about all the physicians you've had throughout your life. Can you specifically link the educational background, grades, or the medical school they attended to the doctor you believe gave you the best or *exemplary* patient care?

How you use and process data can also have an impact on your assumptions about the link between star performance and educational background. For example, although it may be statistically true that an individual with a Harvard MBA may have a higher income than someone who graduated from a public institution with the same degree, we tend to ask a different set of questions. For us, the more relevant question is whether this more "valued" MBA degree directly affects the differences between a *star* performer and a typical performer. Our observation is that these common assumptions about the superiority of educational institutions are not a predictive factor.

Skills and Knowledge

Obviously, superstars possess the requisite skills and knowledge that are required for their role; these are necessary to ensure success. We don't challenge the validity of this assumption, but we do challenge whether or not merely possessing the right skills and knowledge clearly differentiates between a star and average performer.

However, all too often organizations take a "more must be better" approach regarding the skills and knowledge of an individual performer. This assumption is certainly understandable, given that the star performers we encounter in our practice have unique insights about their jobs and clearly do have the *relevant* skills and knowledge to perform successfully. Still, this assumption might even have dangerous consequences if taken to an extreme degree. Here's a somewhat fanciful situation to illustrate our point. Consider for a moment the choice you might make if you began having chest pains, started sweating profusely, and pain was radiating down your left arm. Who would you hope to be close at hand?

- A professor of human physiology;
- A biomedical engineer who had designed an artificial heart; or
- An EMT who had successfully resuscitated 200 heart attack victims.

Our contention is not that additional learning is a bad thing, just that we shouldn't confuse knowing a lot about something with producing the desired result.

Clearly, the first two have lots of knowledge about the human heart and how it works. Both would likely recognize that your symptoms indicated you were having a heart attack. However, if an EMT with such a successful resuscitation track record were available at that moment, we are fairly sure of the choice you'd make. It might reassure you somewhat that the EMT had studied a great deal concerning cardiopulmonary resuscitation and other related subjects. But the bottom line is that you would choose an EMT who has consistently demonstrated the ability to produce the desired result—a patient who survives and thrives after experiencing a heart attack.

Our contention is not that additional learning is a bad thing, just that *we shouldn't confuse knowing a lot about something with producing the desired result*. Our star performers can sometimes explain why something is done a certain way, but not always. More commonly, we observe them doing a procedure or making a decision differently from others, and when we ask them why, these stars often remark that they thought everyone did it the same way or would make the same decision. After all, for these high performers, "it only makes sense to do it that way."

In short, exemplars are very different from those individuals we often call *subject-matter experts* (SMEs). SMEs have the knowledge to explain *why* something is done a certain way and may even be the repository of historical data. Still, even with this abundance of skills and knowledge, the SMEs may be only average performers in terms of consistently producing results that matter for the organization.

Motivation

Motivation is something that we all bring to the job. Prompted to recall their first day on a particular job, most people would remember getting up a little earlier than needed, thinking about what they were going to wear, showing up a little early, and having a bounce in their step as they made their way in to work. Then six months later, management asks why these same people come to work dragging their feet, chin scraping the ground, and no smile on their faces? Was the motivation to do a good job lost? Or was there something in the work environment that was missing (or wrong things present) and the person was no longer quite as excited or engaged? Some say that a person's internal motivation and drive are what sets him or her apart and what makes for star performers. (See Chapter Nine for more on motivation.)

We believe that most people are motivated to do a great job and that typically the work system or organizational culture just gets in the way. From our observations, star performers:

- Define their own standards and derive satisfaction from the outputs they produce and
- Don't necessarily work harder (at "staying motivated") to produce superior results.

In fact, it's very possible to work hard doing the wrong things and to develop "competence" in suboptimal performance by practicing bad habits.

10,000 Hours of Experience

In his book *Outliers: The Story of Success*, the celebrated author and contemporary thinker Malcolm Gladwell popularized his carefully researched concept that it takes at least 10,000 hours of experience or practice to achieve a significant level of expertise.[6]

Gladwell makes his point through descriptions of how famous star performers—including legendary rock bands and Olympic athletes—gained their extraordinary expertise. He pointed out that The Beatles accumulated more live performance experience in Britain and Germany than any other band, just in the few years prior to their coming to the United States.

Olympic gold medal swimming champion Michael Phelps swam close to fifty miles every week, practicing six hours a day, six days a week in the years prior to the 2008 Olympics. This practice regime alone racked up 10,000 hours of practice every five years.

However, simply "showing up" for work and racking up 10,000 hours of on-the-job experience is very different from the concentrated effort put out by musical or athletic stars. Captain

Sullenberger had 19,000 hours of experience prior to his incredible landing in the Hudson River. Clearly, there are other pilots who can match his 19,000 hours of experience, but can we then say that all pilots with 19,000 hours are superstars or potential superstars? If 19,000 hours were some magic number, then we'd simply work to get all pilots to that experience level. If we conclude that exemplary performance is more than simply thousands of hours of experience, then the job is to figure out what sets star performers apart—beyond just having extensive experience.

What Makes Them Tick?

Our experience working with superstars across industries, roles, and even cultures tells us that some commonalities exist. Here are our current working hypotheses:

- Rich mental models
- Clarity of expectations and quality of feedback
- Intentionality
- Mastery and execution of fundamentals
- Leveraging resources optimally

Rich Mental Models

A rich mental model is simply a way of classifying, solving, or thinking about a performance situation or requirement. The following examples will help to explain the concept.

A global high-tech company salesperson working on a sales project explained that his mental model for success was to focus on engagement and to be highly collaborative. The salesperson said that when his aim was to dislodge a competitor, the first step he took was to find an internal advocate within the client organization. He would then give that individual the opportunity to provide feedback that would ultimately have an impact on the final proposed solution. In the end, the internal advocate was an ally who did the selling to the rest of the client organization's internal team.

In an oil refinery, a sophisticated control room is at the heart of the process for turning oil and its derivatives into commercially

Figure 5.3. Control Limit Graph for Petroleum Products

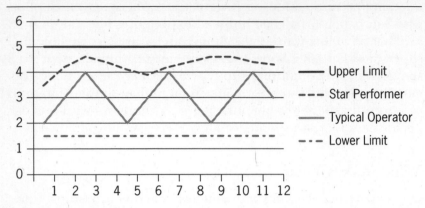

useful products. One of the control room operators consistently produced more of the valued end product per shift than any of the others. The typical operators viewed their jobs as simply making sure nothing went wrong as they monitored gauges and alarms, shifted product flows, and adjusted pressures and temperatures.

The exemplary performer, on the other hand, seemed busier than his counterparts, and we noticed that he also monitored additional gauges. When we observed him, we learned that the key to his success was in finding a leading indicator that allowed him to keep production near the top of the acceptable production ranges (see Figure 5.3). He had learned that this technique increased company profitability. This close monitoring meant that he needed to make adjustments more frequently than his peers did, but he took great satisfaction in helping the company make more product and money during his shift. As a side note, the fact that there was profit sharing among employees is not a trivial point in this example!

Clarity of Expectations and Feedback

In the preceding oil refinery example, the expectation was that the operator should keep the instruments within certain defined tolerances. Knowing that the refinery was a profit-making enterprise was no secret either. Our star performer focused on his own expectations (part of his mental model). Yes, he knew he needed to stay within the specified parameters. He also was keenly aware of the relationship between production and profits. He had an internal drive to challenge himself. Throughout his shift, he had feedback from the instrumentation on how he was doing. The difference was his self-imposed standard to be near the upper limit without ever crossing over—while his coworkers were focused on staying in the perceived safety zone by staying in the exact middle of the upper and lower bounds.

Superstars tend to be accomplishment focused and, therefore, have a clear picture of the goals of their efforts. This clarity of expectations comes from focusing on what they are accomplishing or producing versus simply what they are "doing." With this goal in mind, these star performers are able to more clearly judge whether they are, in fact, producing worthy accomplishments, and they often set their own criteria of what "good" looks like. In turn, the stars develop key performance indicators (KPIs) that are leading, rather than lagging. In addition, these KPIs are often different from those published by the organization. Another value produced by this clarity concerning accomplishments is that there is minimal non-value-added activity. Star performers quickly realize whether doing something will lead to the desired result or not—and they adjust their performance accordingly.

Intentionality

We have all heard the cliché that "practice makes perfect." We update this cliché a bit: *practice makes permanent, but only perfect practice makes perfect*. To illustrate the point, consider how long you have been writing by hand. However, if you took time to write your name on a piece of paper, does the result look like perfect penmanship? Such a poor result (we assume) from a lifetime of practice!

> Practice makes permanent, but only perfect practice makes perfect.

When we observe star performers on the job, we often see people on every shift, like the refinery operator above, who are focused on improving production. Yet, the star operator was able to identify leading indicators using available gauges that other operators did not notice. The star performer exhibited intentionality toward improving his outputs day after day.

Our star examples involve musicians and athletes, because the results are obvious and often well known. At first glance, you may still be tempted to attribute success to raw talent. After all, Michael Phelps is 6′ 4″ tall and has a "wingspan" that is even bigger at 6′ 7″! Phelps wears size 14 shoes, but has relatively short legs. Lance Armstrong has twice the lung capacity of the average man. Certainly, these star athletes do possess some physiological advantages. However, each athlete races against time. When we hear about the athletes' almost unfathomable workouts and realize progress is clocked every lap, we begin to understand the significance of their intentionality. For example, feedback for Michael Phelps comes in 15 discrete measurements for each lap of each race.

Research in the world of musicians also provides significant insight about the role of intentional practice. Anders Ericsson, Conradi Eminent Scholar and Professor of Psychology at Florida State University, tracked the progress of students at the West Berlin Academy, a top music school. Upon graduation, the students ended up in jobs as soloists, symphony performers, and music teachers. The single most important variable that determined the final career destination of the students was directly related to their lifetime practice habits (see Table 5.2). Students who ended up as soloists practiced nearly twice as much as those who became music teachers.

Is there something we can transfer based on our observation of the intentionality of these exemplary performers? For our refinery operator, we can leverage the results of his intentionality by sharing these "leading indicators" with other operators. We can also update the expectations of operators, by showing them the exact

Table 5.2. Ultimate Musical Career by Hours of Practice

Position after graduation	Soloist	Symphony Performer	Music Teacher
Average hours of practice	7,410	5,301	3,420

zones of higher production, so that they can make the linkage between higher production, company revenue, and employee profit sharing. And we can provide job aids (performance support) that equip average operators to model the actions of our star performer.

Deliberate practice is designed to specifically improve performance. It is repeated and the opportunity exists for immediate, corrective feedback. In addition, our experience shows that a coach, mentor, or teacher is often involved in providing both observation and feedback. As you might guess, this practice challenges both the mental and physical resources of those who wish to emulate any star performer—but, of course, that shouldn't be news to anyone.

Mastery and Execution of Fundamentals

Carl Binder defines fluency as the fluid combination of accuracy plus speed that characterizes competent performance.[7] It's worth dwelling on this idea for a moment to underscore a few points. The first is that we are tempted to think about mastery or fluency in terms of accuracy alone. For example, if you provided a mathematics test of 100 simple multiplication problems to solve, you might expect most adults (perhaps even 100%) to get them all correct. However, if you added a time dimension to your test—how long it took each of your test subjects to answer the questions—your data might show a range of 43 seconds to 14 minutes to achieve 100% accuracy.

When reflecting on your "time to completion" data, you would likely conclude that there was something very different about the person who completed the assignment with 100% accuracy in 43 seconds. Clearly, this multiplication whiz was "fluent" in simple multiplication. If your future tax accountant was among the test subjects, you'd be more comfortable if he was closer to the 43 seconds than the 14 minutes. We all have a sense that this would be an important capability in a high-performing accountant.

Exemplary performers in sports, music, and other disciplines devote great amounts of time to practicing fundamentals. We then assume that any unique outcomes of this extensive practice are directly attributable to some other factor, such as a "natural gift." Here's an example. Besides being known for his gifts as a professional golfer, Tiger Woods has demonstrated his ability to bounce a golf ball effortlessly on the end of a golf club. This is not a "natural" gift, but rather a "secondary effect" from spending thousands of hours on the practice tee. According to Tiger, the skill is something he picked up over the years while waiting his turn at the driving range. If he spent that much time (to develop this unique talent) *while waiting* to practice his golf shot, imagine how much time he spent on the driving range, actually hitting golf balls?

> *Star performers tend to be "unconsciously competent" . . . they have trouble accurately describing how they do certain activities.*

Another element of mastery and execution of the fundamentals is "consciousness" while performing an activity. The star performers we interview and observe tend to be "unconsciously competent," which means that they have trouble accurately describing how they do certain activities. Their mastery is so refined that they no longer "think" about it; in other words, the activity has become "second nature."

When a performer's mind is freed from thinking about all the details of a task, it frees up capacity to think about better ways of monitoring the function, checking it, and adjusting performance in real time. To illustrate, think about your experience of learning to drive a car. Your mind was probably focused on executing the fundamentals. Your "brain power" was fully devoted to accuracy and executing these fundamentals in the right order. When you approached a stop sign, you lifted your foot off the accelerator, then depressed the brakes (but not too hard), and came to a full stop. If you were signaling a turn, you likely looked down to find the turn signal. Today, you don't look down to see where the signal arm is—you know where it is instinctively. You are able to keep your eyes on the road more consistently, and this translates into better awareness of the conditions outside your car (actions of other drivers, road conditions, signs, and so on). Even if you buy a new car and some of the controls are in a slightly different location, you are much better prepared to take note of these differences, make the internal adjustments, and rapidly regain your fluency of driving.

Another characteristic of exemplary performers is that they tend to acquire mastery of execution and fundamentals faster than other performers. In addition, once star performers acquire mastery, they are better able to shift this energy and brainpower to achieving something else. Recall our refinery operator who was able to master staying between the control limit lines. He felt this was relatively easy to do. Once he had mastered this aspect of the job, he was able to shift his thinking to accomplishing something of even greater value—higher production and great profits for his company.

Leveraging Resources Optimally

Another key attribute of star performers is that they leverage resources extremely well; that is, they know how to make the best use of the tools available to them. Here's another example from our practice that happens to also come from an oil refinery project.

"Outside operators" have the somewhat frightening job of climbing the towers out on the process units in order to take in-person readings of gauges. These workers also transfer chemicals and petroleum products from one tank to another and respond to other problems that may arise. In many ways, they are the lifeblood of an oil refinery.

We had asked a star performer to "walk us through" the procedure for transferring catalyst from one holding tank to another. This catalyst has a fine sand consistency and is heated to temperatures approaching 800° F and is used to help break down oil into other products (such as gasoline and other petroleum products). A simplified drawing of the set-up of tanks, valves, and piping looked something like the diagram in Figure 5.4.

The official procedure for transferring catalyst from Tank 1 to Tank 2 read: "*slowly open valve A partially to allow catalyst to flow through valve B.*" Our first question was whether valves C, D, and E should be opened or closed as part of the procedure. The answer was that these valves did not function and were always left in the open position. Next, we asked what the terms *slowly* and *partially* meant in the official procedure instructions. What does partially mean? How much do you open the valve? Answer: Enough to let

Figure 5.4. Diagram of Catalyst Transfer

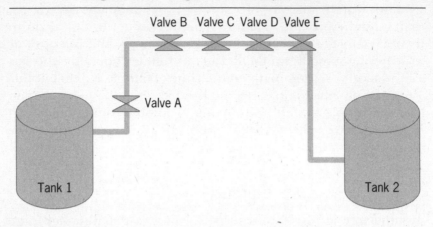

the catalyst flow from Tank 1 to Tank 2, but slowly enough so that it is about 300°F when it passes through valve B. In Tank 1 the catalyst is about 800°F. If you open the valve too much, it will flow too fast and be at a temperature that will melt vital parts of valve B. If you open it too little, a 20-minute job will take 2 hours. We asked if this had been a problem in the past. Answer: Yes, that's why valves C, D, and E are no longer functional. How much does a valve cost to replace? $45,000.

The next question to our star performer was: How do you know when the temperature going through valve B is approximately 300°F? The answer: Oh, I use this infrared gun—you just point it at the valve and it will give you a readout of the temperature. (This is essentially the same technology and operation as that of an ear thermometer.)

Once those questions were answered, it was a very straight-forward, even simple procedure. Our next question was about whether everyone else knew about the infrared gun. At first our star performer said, "Of course," and then, staring at the three nonfunctioning valves, he said, "Well, I guess not." In fact, we had asked other operators about this and most did not know about the infrared gun or the specific temperature that valve B would tolerate. How did this operator know this so well? His past experience had been in the Navy nuclear submarine pro-gram, including coursework on thermodynamics. The refinery didn't buy the infrared gun for this purpose. It could have put a temperature gauge near valve B and perhaps obtained similar results. Based on his previous experience, the star performer had a different mental model. He knew how he could measure the temperature from a distance, using an infrared device, and was able to leverage the available resources of the refinery.

Summary: The Exemplary Performance System (EPS) Model

As you have seen in this chapter, providing the ingredients for creating exemplary performers is difficult. You can't shut down a business for years in order to realize the benefits of intentionality and 10,000 hours of directed practice. And it's certainly impractical to conclude that you should just concentrate on hiring star performers like the examples we have offered in this chapter. Our refinery example of the former Navy submarine sailor using an infrared device hits dead center. Can the oil refinery hire such people exclusively? No. But the refinery can leverage the insights and mental models that have been developed and proven successful by their own star performers in a systematic way so that others at the refinery can obtain the same results (in this case, not damaging $45,000 valves).

In his book *Improving Performance: How to Manage the White Space in the Organizational Chart*, organizational development and human performance expert Geary Rummler noted: *"If you pit a good person against a bad system, the system wins every time."*[8]

With that in mind, let's start with a good system, one designed for producing exemplary performance. The EPS Model is depicted in Figure 5.5.

Clearly, the path to increasing the number of people who drive results (like the stars in your organization) is found by leveraging the insights and mental models that have been developed and proven successful by the existing exemplary performers—and doing so in a systematic way. That's the purpose of Part Two of this book: to show you how to attend to each of the factors in the EPS Model in a deliberate way, gained from observing star performers in their roles and architecting a system with the right ingredients found in each of the model's arrows.

Figure 5.5. Exemplary Performance Systems Model

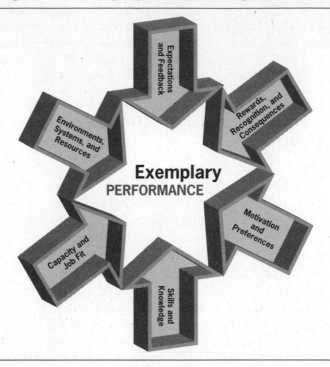

Source: Exemplary Performance, LLC. Copyright 2008–2012.

Notes

1. Chesley Sullenberger, Interview on *60 Minutes*, CBS News, February 8, 2009. http://www.cbsnews.com/2100–18560_162–4764852.html
2. E. Michaels, H. Handfield-Jones, and B. Axelrod, *The War for Talent* (Boston: Harvard Business School Publishing, 2001).
3. Ibid.
4. Sales Executive Council, "Shifting the Performance Curve," Executive Briefing (Washington, DC: Corporate Executive Board, 2003).
5. Geoff Colvin, *Talent Is Overrated: What Really Separates World-Class Performers from Everybody Else* (New York: Penguin, 2010).
6. Malcolm Gladwell, *Outliers: The Story of Success* (New York: Penguin, 2008).
7. C. Binder, "Behavioral Fluency: Evolution of a New Paradigm," *The Behavior Analyst*, 19, no. 2 (1996): 163–197.
8. Geary Rummler and Alan Brache, *Improving Performance: Managing the White Space on the Organizational Chart* (San Francisco: Jossey-Bass, 1995).

PART TWO

Shifting the
Performance Curve

CHAPTER SIX

Leading for Exceptional Results

This chapter introduces Part Two: Shifting the Performance Curve. The next six chapters are designed to equip you with the tools you will need as a manager to shift the performance curve of your team or organization. This section is a natural segue from the first section, where we showed you how to prioritize your performance improvement efforts, identify true exemplary performers, and create models of optimal performance for critical team or organizational roles. Now let's look at some key questions for you to consider as you read this section:

- How can I, as a manager, use this approach to drive greater results with my direct reports?
- How can I, as a leader, leverage star performers across the enterprise, to gain strategic advantage?

The weak link between organizational strategy and results is execution. Managers are chided that they need to think strategically; however, establishing a strategy does not equate to improved results. Often those who recognize the powerful and important impact of sound strategy lack either the focus or commitment to bring that strategy to fruition. In their book *Execution*, Bossidy and Charon (2002) emphasize that leaders are not taught the discipline of execution, nor is it part of most executive development programs.[1] That's an unfortunate state of affairs, because a large part of the answer as to what is needed to drive real performance improvement is found by viewing the valued results of an organization as an output of the entire work system.

> *Star performers either view their work environment as a system—or they create that system—to produce the results that bring value to the organization.*

Part One of this book provided you with an alternative model for driving your business forward based on shifting the performance curve. However, there is tremendous value in capturing the current star performers' mental models and leveraging that with incumbents to accelerate performance.

We have examined star performers from the vantage of how they become stars. Now we want to consider how stars look at things once they have "arrived." Star performers either view their work environment as a system—or they create that system—to produce the results that bring value to the organization. In Part Two, we want to shift your thinking from what makes a star performer to what it takes to be an exemplary manager. Our research and experience tell us that exemplary managers create work systems that enable their organizations to perform at exceptionally high levels. To do this you need to align six distinct subsystems (see Figure 6.1):

- Expectations and Feedback
- Rewards, Recognition, and Consequences
- Motivation and Preferences
- Skills and Knowledge
- Capacity and Job Fit
- Environments, Systems, and Resources

Figure 6.1. Exemplary Performance System Model

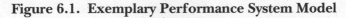

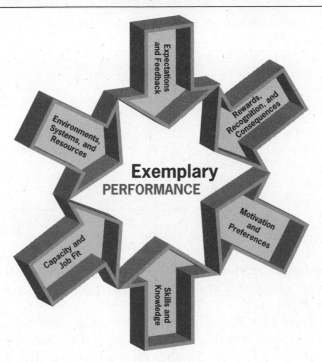

The Power of Systems Thinking

Joel Salatin is a farmer in the Shenandoah Valley who certainly qualifies as an exemplary performer. He is the author of numerous books, has been featured on the front page of *USA Today*, and has been called "America's Most Influential Farmer." His family farm is very profitable; his farm products demand premium prices; and his methods are both sustainable and innovative. Yet we highlight the accomplishments of Mr. Salatin here for a more "behind the scenes" reason; he is also a star at systems integration. Here's why.

When we first met Joel, it was mid-July in Swoope, Virginia. He asked us whether we noticed anything peculiar as we approached his farm. Not being full-time farmers, let alone experts in farming, nothing special had grabbed our attention. He then asked if we noticed that neighboring farms were feeding their cattle hay and that their fields were brown? Yes, we did notice that. He then went

Figure 6.2. Growth Rate of Grasses

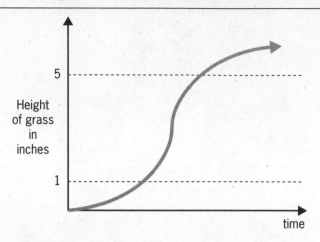

to a chalkboard and provided two lessons. The first was about the growth rate of grasses, which has an S-shaped growth pattern, as shown in Figure 6.2.

Joel explained that when cattle are permitted to eat grass down to the dirt, it takes a relatively long time for the grass to recover to the one-inch height. After getting to the one-inch height, it grows quite rapidly to about five or six inches, and will then slow its growth again. Anyone who lives in an area where he or she has to mow the lawn weekly will acknowledge there must be some truth to this.

The second lesson Mr. Salatin gave us was that, left on their own, cattle will eat grass down to the soil. Most farmers will put cattle in large fields and allow the cattle to feed on grass until it's gone. The farmers are then forced to feed the cattle hay, which is more expensive. Joel found that by subdividing his fields into smaller sections and rotating the cattle from one area to the next—prior to them baring the soil—he could keep the grass in that rapid growth range and keep his cattle fed on grass longer into the summer, before switching over to more expensive hay. But as Joel pointed out for us, the benefits accrue to other areas of his business as well.

As it turns out, Joel found that these just-vacated fields were a perfect place for his free-range chickens. Not only did they thrive in the open space, but they would also claw through the manure, looking for bugs. Some farmers object to the smaller fields, because it is extra work to move the cattle so frequently. Joel maintained that it is worth the effort, because of the money saved from not feeding hay. And while the chickens' actions serve as "manure spreaders," they ultimately eliminate fly and other insect problems. Other farmers typically use machinery to first collect and then spread manure. And they spend time and money with the use of insecticides. Meanwhile, regulations in much of the United States require that "free-range chickens" are those that have at least eight square feet of space per chicken. When chickens follow the cattle into the open field, they get hundreds of square feet of space (probably closer to what you and I think "free range" really means). In addition, when chickens get this much space, grass, and fresh air, their need for antibiotics goes away. Did you know that typical henhouse chickens are fed a *daily* dose of antibiotics? Joel has written the book *Salad Bar Beef*, about the cattle that eat "natural" grasses versus hay and corn (to fatten them up near the end).[2] Meanwhile his chickens demand higher prices than cooped or typical free-range chickens.

Worth is defined as the value of accomplishments minus the cost of producing those outputs:

$$W = V - C$$

Interesting information, right? So why have we used the story about Joel Salatin, a farmer, as the introduction to Part Two? Because while Joel is a farmer, he is also a systems thinking guru. This farmer produces outputs of value (chickens and cattle for the market). If the system were suboptimized, he would still be producing those two outputs, but at a higher cost and at a lower value. Worth is defined as the value of the accomplishments minus the cost of producing those outputs. We can imagine a situation in which Joel doesn't use the chickens as natural manure spreaders and insect devourers, and has to use machinery to collect and then spread manure on his fields. That raises the cost of producing the outputs. His cattle would then need antibiotics and insecticides because of the insect issues. In the marketplace this would result in lower prices for his beef. The chickens could be cooped up, and therefore need antibiotics and additional feed. He could still ensure they received their allotted eight square feet per chicken, but both the value (premium price consumers pay for the chicken) and the cost to produce the output (cost of feed) would move in directions that were unfavorable to his organization.

Why Execution Is So Important

Execution really begins in the first part of this book, when we align the accomplishments of people with the organization's goals and then identify exemplary performers. What we learn from those exemplary performers directly connects to the management activities described in the next six chapters. If you started with a blank sheet of paper and designed organizational positions (jobs, roles), while attending to each of the six arrows in the Exemplary Performance System Model (see Figure 6.1), you would be off to a great start. Here's what we mean:

Expectations and Feedback: Providing clear expectations and feedback is not just a good idea—it is essential for any performer. To optimize this component, you need accomplishments and excellence indicators (KPIs) from the star performers in order to capture important details that differentiate the stars from average performers.

Rewards, Recognition, and Consequences: You don't want to provide rewards and incentives in an arbitrary manner or in a way that rewards effort alone, but rather in a way that is aligned with the value produced for the organization by people. Before rewarding effort, you must ensure that effort is aligned in the proper direction.

Motivation and Preferences: Understanding the exemplary performers' motivation and preferences allows you to align the recognition and rewards more tightly and eliminate or at least minimize the negative influences on the job.

Skills and Knowledge: Accomplishment-based curriculum design provides efficient and high-fidelity simulation for producing required job outputs. When training is designed without clarity of accomplishments in sight, the training is often generalized to the point where it provides awareness, but not proficiency—and the cost for such training is excessive.

Capacity and Job Fit: An understanding of the outputs produced by your star performers allows you to clarify job descriptions and hiring actions that reflect real job expectations. This hiring clarity enables you to decide on candidates, not by trusting the reliability of weak instruments to measure potential, but rather by evidence of whether a person has successfully produced analogous outputs required by the organization for this particular role.

Environments, Systems, and Resources: You need to discern why exemplary performers have succeeded in the midst of existing barriers and use their experience to remove, design away, or mitigate such impediments.

Exemplary Performance System (EPS) and "Face Validity"

Once managers are exposed to the EPS model, they agree it makes sense and has "face validity." In other words, it is very clear that insights from star performers are required to truly optimize each component of the system. Could you ignore the Profile of Exemplary Performance you created when you are on-boarding a new hire, attend to the other elements in Part Two, and still end up with a high-performing organization? Yes, *but* it would be suboptimized. And suboptimal results don't drive your organization to exemplary success!

The key to optimizing both individual and organizational success is to manage the top three arrows of the model (which belong to the organization) even before hiring. Then attend to the bottom three arrows of the model (which belong to the individual performer) during and after hiring (or reassignment). The following chapters provide you with a specific "how-to" strategy to accomplish this goal.

The question becomes: How do you go about actually leveraging what it is that your star performers do that produces such stunning results? As a critically time-constrained manager, you may be tempted to say you couldn't possibly manage these six areas in a deliberate way. A lasting principle we got from systems guru and low-tech farmer Joel Salatin is this: "Never let your chores take up more than four hours a day. Otherwise, you won't have enough time to tinker" (his code word for *innovate*). Most farmers don't think this way, nor do most managers. Can you afford not to?

Notes

1. Larry Bossidy and Ram Charon, *Execution* (New York: Crown Business, 2002).
2. Joel Salatin, *Salad Bar Beef* (Swoope, VA: Polyface Farms, Inc., 1996).

CHAPTER SEVEN

You Get What You Expect and What You Inspect

Figure 7.1. The Role of Expectations and Feedback in the EPS Model

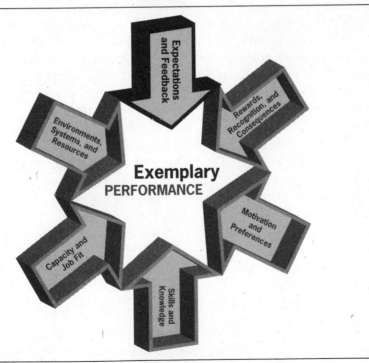

Source: Exemplary Performance, LLC. Copyright 2008–2012.

> **In This Chapter**
>
> ---
>
> - The Power of Expectations
> - Feedback: Breakfast of Champions
> - Effective Coaching
> - Case Studies

The Power of Expectations

Figure 7.1 shows the relationship of expectations to exemplary performance and other factors we have discussed. Clear expectations matter. Research has shown that the greatest source of substandard performance is a lack of clear expectations and feedback. Too often, overreacting to concerns of being "micromanagers," managers have abdicated their responsibilities and left direct reports with the "autonomy" to figure things out on their own. At best, such an approach provides vague expectations and untimely feedback, if any. In what was startling research in 1968 and remains controversial to this day, Harvard professor Robert Rosenthal and elementary school principal Lenore Jacobson repeatedly demonstrated the power of expectations in the classroom.[1] By convincing teachers that their students were gifted, the teachers' expectations for those students became elevated, and in subsequent measures, including grades, standardized test scores and even IQ exams, the students' scores all rose significantly.

This "Pygmalion effect" has also been demonstrated in the corporate environment. J. Sterling Livingston, in *Pygmalion in Management*,[2] came to the following conclusions:

A unique characteristic of superior managers is the ability to create high performance expectations, in turn, subordinates fulfill.

- What managers expect of subordinates and the way they treat them largely determine subordinate performance and subsequent career progress.
- A unique characteristic of superior managers is the ability to create high performance expectations that, in turn, subordinates fulfill.

- Less effective managers fail to develop similar high expectations, and as a consequence, the productivity of their subordinates suffers.

From this and other confirming research, here are two separate manager and subordinate scenarios that demonstrate the power of a positive, high-expectation message, one involving a manager with a high level of self-confidence and another from a manager with just an average level of self-confidence.

Manager with high self-confidence: A self-confident manager believes in his judgment and ability to make good choices. This manager believes his subordinates will succeed and even excel in the jobs given them by virtue of the manager's instinctual abilities to pick winners. The subordinate working for this manager takes his or her high-expectation directions from the manager's aura of self-confidence and expectation of success. *If I picked you and you work for me—then you will do great.*

Manager with average self-confidence: Even a manager with less self-confidence who nonetheless finds a reason to believe the subordinate is superior can communicate these high expectations. *I just know you will do great!*

Clearly, both managers communicate high expectations effectively to their subordinates. The difference is the rationale or source of the manager's confidence in the subordinate's ability to succeed.

The Miracle of High Expectations

Dr. James Sweeny was a professor of industrial management and psychiatry at Tulane University[3] in the 1960s who believed he could teach even a poorly educated person to operate and program computers at the Biomedical Computer Center at Tulane (a facility he also managed for the university). To prove his point, he selected a janitor named George Johnson. Sweeny began teaching Johnson about computers in the afternoons, following Johnson's completion of janitorial duties each morning. In the midst of this effort, the university set a minimum IQ standard for various positions, including that of computer operator and programmer. Johnson was tested and his IQ results implied he was not even capable of learning how to type, much less become a computer operator and programmer. Sweeny threatened to quit unless allowed to continue his project. Sweeny (and Johnson) prevailed—and Johnson went on to be in charge of the main computer room and responsible for training new employees how to operate and program the computers.

Of course, the story of a janitor turned computer programmer and trainer as a result of high expectations is unusual, but nonetheless makes a good point. As noted in the next example, a great amount of research has also been done on the impact of high expectations in a more typical work environment.

Self-Fulfilling Expectations at Work

Managers' expectations of subordinates can also have a powerful effect on overall productivity in the workplace. More recent research by Dr. Dov Eden of Tel Aviv University supports the assertion that when managers communicate high expectations to their subordinates, the result is greater workplace productivity. Eden concluded that elevated expectations did in fact lay the foundation for positive results. He notes that these expectations unleash "dormant energy in the workplace by harnessing the Pygmalion effect and other self-fulfilling prophecies processes."[4] High expectations do more than create positive work environments; expecting more has a significant impact on organizational performance.

The Role of Nonverbal Communication

As noted earlier, much of the Pygmalion effect comes from a manager's nonverbal communication and the messages of genuine confidence that are projected to the subordinate. The manager communicates high expectations for the subordinate, who finds the assignment challenging, yet most likely achievable. Additionally, the subordinate must believe the manager's confidence is genuine. In the research experiment for *Pygmalion in the Classroom*, teachers were told they had a group of *gifted* children.

> *High expectations do more than create positive work environments; expecting more has a significant impact on organizational performance.*

Therefore, they had reason to expect remarkable achievements by their students. They communicated these high expectations to the students, and the students delivered. However, the children in the study were randomly assigned to the gifted group and, in reality, were average students.

When we identify high standards based on what exemplary performers are already doing, we can provide expectations about something that is achievable and not simply "pie in the sky." The question that arises, however, is: Can a manager truly develop such high confidence in his or her direct reports? To summarize the logic flow, consider the following:

- Is the work under discussion described in terms of the accomplishments produced by people who provide value to the organization? This establishes both relevance and value, and connects to the basic motivation of people to do well.
- Are the standards and associated criteria for the work drawn from what is currently being produced by exemplary performers in the same organization, in the same organizational culture, and in the same work environment? This establishes that the work and associated standards are achievable.
- Do the specifics of the work (outputs, standards, criteria) equip the manager to have a specific conversation with the direct reports? This means that the up-front expectations have specificity that improves the dialogue between manager and direct report, so each has confidence that the message communicated and received is the same.
- Is feedback concerning the work based on the same set of standards and criteria used to communicate the original expectations? This increases the "fairness" of corrective feedback and also improves the likelihood that those areas requiring correction will actually be corrected.
- Do the other five elements of the EPS Model provide support and thus bolster confidence?

Means of Communicating Expectations

As noted, expectations are transmitted through either verbal or nonverbal pathways. In addition to their supervisor or manager, employees receive organizational expectations from a variety of sources, both formal and informal. These are listed below and then explained in more detail:

- Policies and procedures.
- Job aids and training materials
- Organizational culture
- Recognition systems

Policies and Procedures

Organizations create and promulgate a variety of official policies and procedures, which sometimes communicate behavioral norms for the organization or describe how to accomplish specific types of work. Sometimes policy statements are posted in workplaces just to ensure compliance with government regulation or are created to avoid lawsuits. But when you find icons on the computer desktop, favorites in the browser, and dog-eared pages in readily accessible manuals, you have discovered indicators of policies and procedures that are truly in effect and meaningful for your organization.

Job Aids and Training Materials

Training materials and job aids should be by-products of approved policy and procedure. Too often we find the official policy or procedure is out of date or nonexistent. Trainers in organizations are rightly wary of having their materials become the "official" way of doing things out in the workplace in the absence of approved policy. At other times we hear of supervisors telling their just-back-from-training employees that the way they learned to do something in training is not the way things are done around here.

Organizational Culture

"How things are done around here" is great shorthand for explaining organizational culture. Unquestionably, culture dictates expectations. Comments like "Yes, we have an official procedure, but no one follows it" speak volumes. Does an organization truly have a safety culture? Start to enter an area that requires a hardhat and hearing protection without wearing this protective equipment. Does anyone stop you and correct you? When we see entry-level people, experienced people, and those in supervisory positions all attentive to safety precautions, there obviously is a safety culture. When supervisors take shortcuts and are not confronted, it's quite likely others take shortcuts and safety is only a slogan and not part of the culture. Either way, expectations are set—good or bad.

Recognition Systems

> The goal in setting expectations should be to have alignment with organizational priorities, consistency among means of communication, and clarity of message.

Recognition systems (discussed in detail in Chapter Eight) also communicate organizational priorities and expectations. If, on the one hand, bonus structures are tied to meeting certain priorities, employees will respond accordingly. On the other hand, if the reward for exemplary work is simply more work, then employees are unlikely to have a great interest in meeting an organization's priorities and expectations.

The goal in setting expectations should be to have alignment with organizational priorities, consistency among means of communication, and clarity of message. If there is disagreement between formal and informal communications, then changes need to be made.

Feedback: Breakfast of Champions

The quote "feedback is the breakfast of champions" is attributed to Ken Blanchard, perhaps best known for *The One Minute Manager* and *Situational Leadership*. Whether athlete, musician, or knowledge worker, the cycle of performance (perform, feedback, revise, perform) holds true as the means to improve results. In Chapter Five we examined feedback from the vantage point of the exemplary performer, who practices long hours with intentionality and receives continuous feedback. Here we examine feedback from a different vantage point, which is about how to *provide* useful, effective, results-oriented feedback.

Motorola conducted a study of the return on investment from training and found that training returned $33 for every $1 invested in plants where the training was followed with *on-the-job feedback* once the workers returned to their jobs.[5] In plants where no feedback occurred, the study showed there was actually a negative return on investment. Commenting about the plants where no feedback occurred, Motorola University president William Wiggenhorn pointed out: "Workers began to wonder why they'd taken the training. They learned how to keep a Pareto chart and make an Ishikawa diagram, but no one ever appeared on the floor and asked to see one."[6] The bottom line was that, even though the stated corporate priority was quality improvement, some managers still conveyed an expectation of production at all costs. Even after workers were trained on quality, the training was not reinforced on the job.

How to Build Feedback Systems

Constructing a feedback system that delivers the power to obtain higher levels of performance requires more detail than determining whether feedback is happening or not. We've discussed the power of nonverbal, optimistic, and confident expectations. Expectations and feedback are two sides of the same coin. People want to do a good job; sometimes it's just unclear to them what "good" looks like. Author Steve Weiss, writing about the feedback provided by Steve Jobs to people at Apple, had this to say: "Despite [his] choice of words, lack of empathy, and sometimes prickly demeanor, he spent a huge amount of time giving his most talented employees constant, hard, critical feedback."[7] Beyond the rough approach is the underlying message of the nonverbal communication to each recipient that "the top guy at Apple is spending time to provide feedback; it is communicating that what I am doing is critically important."

We firmly believe that the greatest organizational ROI comes from helping the B-players perform more like A-players.

The message here mirrors our own Exemplary Performance System approach. Steve Jobs was not spending his time coaching the performers operating in the bottom 20% of the organization. We firmly believe that the greatest organizational ROI comes from helping the B-players (those in the middle) perform more like A-players (those at the top).

Providing Effective Feedback

The macro process for delivering effective feedback begins with collecting information about the accomplishments (or outputs) that people produce on the job, from the vantage point of your organization's exemplary performers. At the same time, collect information about the standards and criteria that exemplary performers use to judge their own work outputs. (See the case studies at the end of this chapter.) The second step is to construct a feedback system that you can use to deliver useful feedback as part of coaching individuals and teams.

Precision of Expectations and Feedback

One of the most important aspects in collecting data from exemplary performers is specificity. You want to be precise about how work outputs can be judged. Terms such as "several," "rapidly," "near the center," or "acceptable" are too vague and don't provide the clarity required to improve performance. Table 7.1 offers some criteria for judging and categorizing accomplishments.

Table 7.1. Precision of Accomplishment Criteria

Category of Criteria	Examples
1. Rate or quantity	Number of sales per quarter
	Number of patients seen per day
	Percentage of maintenance agreements sold, following initial sales
2. Quality, accuracy, completeness	Customer alerted to arrival time
	Operating within limits
	In-store theft less than 1% of gross
3. Safety	No patients injured due to faulty technique
	Required PPE worn at all times

Elements of Effective Feedback

The focus of your feedback should be on the work *outputs and not just the behavior or activity*. Once you have clarity about the outputs and associated criteria and standards, the remaining elements include:

- The feedback system allows the employee to discriminate between standard and nonstandard performance.
- Standards are written down, preferably in graphic form.
- Feedback follows soon after the performance (that is, soon after the production of the output). The longer the span between the completion of an output and feedback, the less effective the feedback. Ideally, the feedback should come immediately after the accomplishment is produced and within the same day, if practical. Usually, this is fertile ground for improving performance, as too often feedback is either delayed (by weeks or months) or is completely absent.
- When the accomplishment is below standard, the feedback should come immediately *before* the next opportunity to produce the output.
- Feedback is provided on a regular, ongoing basis.
- Feedback is accompanied by positive consequences.
- Corrective feedback (about the process or behavior) is provided and timely.
- When the feedback system, as described above, is in place, execution is still required. That is, managers and supervisors still have to carry out their responsibilities to make it work.

Effective Coaching

Feedback and coaching are the actions that link an effective feedback system to the results of improved performance. The following list shows the steps of effective coaching:

- *Time*: Provide coaching before the person (or team) produces the output again. Ideally, this should occur immediately before the output will be produced, with no work-related activities in between.

- *Privacy*: If possible, give corrective feedback and coaching in private.
- *Praise*: Reinforce even incremental improvement with praise or recognition.
- *Standards*: Remind the person (or team) of the standards for the output.
- *Compare*: Show a comparison of an output that meets the standard versus a deficient output. If not feasible, describe the two, emphasizing the difference.
- *Demonstrate*: Model (as applicable) the correct actions in small increments.
- *Practice*: Have the person (or team) demonstrate the increment with you observing.
  - If correct—say something like: "Good. That was correct. Let's move on to the next steps …"
  - If not correct, say something like: "That wasn't exactly right. I'd better go over that again. Notice I did this …"
- *Perform*: Observe the process in the job situation to determine whether your corrective feedback and coaching were effective.

Situational Leadership

Ken Blanchard and Paul Hersey developed a leadership framework called "Situational Leadership."[8] The framework suggests using one of four leadership styles (S1 through S4) based on the willingness and ability (called maturity level and development level in variations of their model) of the performer for a particular task or assignment. For the manager, the S1 style is high on providing task behavior and low on relationship behavior, whereas the S4 style is high on relationship and low on task behavior. An underlying aspect of their research is that leaders have a comfort zone style, one that is natural for them. We see this played out in the work setting as a function not only of individual personality, but also as a result of the work environment.

For instance, in high-tech organizations, some managers are not only managers but also are expected to continue as individual contributors. Their success and career progression come mainly from their individual contributions and not from developing people. The temptation for these managers is to either provide excruciatingly detailed feedback (and criticism) or to simply take over difficult projects.

The contrast to this situation is the manager who oversees high-tech workers and does not share the same background and experience and, therefore, finds it nearly impossible to provide specific feedback. In both scenarios these managers (and their organizations) benefit from the use of Profiles of Exemplary Performance (PEP), where the outputs of value are identified as well as the criteria, task sequence, influences, and appropriate performance support.

For the individual contributor/manager with this PEP in hand, the performance discussion with direct reports can stay at a high level, providing clarity on the accomplishments and the criteria about how those outputs will be judged. If the direct report seeks additional detail, the conversation can continue along that path. For the nontechnical manager, the role profile provides details about the work outputs that matter, along with criteria and other details that have been validated by the best performers. Whether providing up-front performance expectations or after-the-fact feedback, the manager is prepared to provide sufficient detail to the conversation.

Another aspect of Situational Leadership is that the manager's style is not only adjusted based on the subordinate's readiness level, but specifically to the subordinate's readiness level for a particular task. To illustrate this idea, Table 7.2 is a partial list of the major accomplishments for a *new* salesperson at ACME Manufacturing and Sales.

For this example, let's say that the new salesperson knows the market and has demonstrated the ability to produce most of the major accomplishments shown above at former companies. Here are some assumptions you might make:

- As the salesperson is new to ACME, using the company's software for generating sales reports is a new or at least different output.
- Most likely the manager will need only to inspect the other accomplishments and provide confirming feedback.
- On the other hand, the importance of providing clarity of expectations, coaching, and corrective feedback may not

Table 7.2. ACME Manufacturing and Sales

Major Accomplishment	Standard
Purchase agreements from customers	Completed correctly with all contact information, payment terms, and signature
List of potential customers	Sufficient to generate 20 sales calls per week over next 2 months
Sales reports from ACME financial systems	Contains previous week's sales data
	Shows trends compared to goals
	Shows fulfillment rates
	Shows return rate

only be necessary for generating "sales reports from ACME financial systems," but will also need to be provided more frequently than the feedback for the outputs produced to standard.

Inspecting

The first elements you should inspect about a job are the outputs, judging those outputs against the criteria and standards that were established at the onset. In a diagnostic way, your inspection should continue if you find the outputs deficient. Your mental model of providing positive expectations leads you to first suspect that the cause of the deficiency has come from one of the following:

- Were clear expectations provided?
- Was the feedback mechanism deficient?
- Was the work environment a barrier to success (see Chapter Nine for more detail)?
- Were the rewards and incentives misaligned, unfair, or unclear?
- Did the person or team who did *not* produce the outputs to standard *not* have the skills and knowledge needed? Were the required training or job aids needed for doing the work either missing or of insufficient quality?

- Was the person or team the wrong individual or team for the work? Was capacity of the individual insufficient to perform the work? (For example, the person says, "I realize I'm just not cut out for working in an office environment," or "I can't stand being in sales," or "being around all the noise and machinery is just too unsettling for me." See Chapter Eleven for more detail.)
- Did the person or team lack the motivation to do a good job? (We find this a rare occurrence. This might be the suspicion based on certain observations, but the cause is typically one of the above reasons that manifest into the appearance of a lack of motivation. For example, a job site that lacks adequate safety equipment and protective clothing might result in some workers not going outside to take readings and instead fudging the number in a logbook. See Chapter Ten for more detail.)

Process Industry Example

Process industries (chemical, petroleum, energy, and so on) are heavily regulated. Some of this regulation requires formal documentation for how things are done. This is also part of industry-specific ISO 29001. Procedures are established, reviewed, documented, approved, and required for use. Following execution of a particular procedure, operators sign paper copies of the procedures, which are then kept on file.

In one project, we informed the plant manager that certain procedures were not being followed as written. To resolve the issue in a productive way, we walked him through what had led up to this point. First, the procedures were outdated and had not been reviewed within the regulatory standards. Second, there were often an insufficient number of people available to perform the procedure as currently written and the procedure was also inefficient. Workers had figured out better ways to accomplish the work.

The manager was correctly concerned that the official procedures were not being followed. He was also justified in his concern that his workers were following new, undocumented, unapproved procedures. We had him go out to the worksite and observe the new procedure to validate that it was proper, safe, and yes, better than the approved procedure on file. The result was a revised and approved procedure that reflected the insights of his exemplary performers. Another outcome was more frequent inspections by this manager—not to catch workers doing something wrong, but rather to ensure they had proper equipment, that procedures were still reasonable and relevant, and to listen for better ways of accomplishing the work.

Expectations and the EPS Model

In our EPS model, influences on performance are nondiscrete; that is, there are spillover and interaction among the categories. For example, clarity of expectations has an impact on job fit,

The first question to ask when getting at the root cause of any deficiency is: Were clear expectations provided?

and this connection begins with the degree of clarity provided when a job is advertised and whether it contains what will *really* be expected. When you provide clarity about what will make someone successful in role, it is easy to see how this will align and energize a person's motivation.

With these connections in mind, imagine providing a checklist with the criteria to evaluate a worker's outputs—and providing this up front, before the work is begun. Later on, imagine using the same checklist to evaluate the person's performance.

Here's our set of guidelines for putting together this "before and after" checklist:

- Did you identify the performance outputs that provide value to the organization?
- Does this checklist capture the mental models, tasks, and criteria around how your best performers produce these outputs?
- Does it set positive and clear expectations for people in the role, sharing these internal best practices?
- Are the expectations communicated with confidence that your people will succeed? (That is, confidence in yourself as manager, confidence in your people that they will succeed, and

confidence drawn from the fact that these are proven practices and not theoretical or flavor of the month.)

- Did you inspect how things were going—using the same criteria you established up front?
- Did you provide feedback with a frequency that is appropriate to each individual—and with specificity?

Summary

The dramatic impact of the Pygmalion effect can be hard to comprehend. However, providing clarity of expectations to people before they do the work, coaching their performance along the way, and then evaluating their outputs according to the same standards and criteria (provided at the outset) is a logical and effective framework. Providing positive and clear expectations is powerful in and of itself, but clearly has linkages to other aspects of the EPS model; knowing what you need to do to be successful is motivating! Providing coaching and feedback develops and hones the recipient's job-relevant skills and knowledge. The next chapter focuses on the role of rewards and incentives as reinforcement for doing the right things.

Case Study: Example of Outputs and Criteria for a Business Unit Director

At upper levels of management, the idea of daily face-to-face contact between "managers of managers" and direct reports is often impractical. In the case below, the director of the business unit was a direct report of a corporate vice president, located in a different state. Table 7.3 shows a "scorecard" that was developed for those in the director role and contains the major accomplishments expected of each director to produce, as well as the standards for each of these outputs.

With scorecard in hand, the corporate VP can have regular discussions that include coaching and feedback about each one of the listed output areas. Examples of outputs that meet the standard and those that do not can easily be shared with direct reports. As an example, the major accomplishment of "Strategic and Tactical Plans" may be vague or subject to varied interpretation by some business unit directors. Rather than trying to explain (or leave it up to interpretation), the CVP can share examples of the best strategic and tactical plans and use these as a starting point in the conversation.

Table 7.3. Major Accomplishments of Business Unit Directors

Major Accomplishments	Criteria
P&L statement for business unit	Achieved corporate goals, across lines of business
Strategic and tactical plans	Tailored to sub-regions, energized across function
Culture of innovation	Portfolio of past, current, and future projects
Highly productive, engaged, and informed workforce	MBOs aligned; employee satisfaction scores; corporate business execution award criteria
Succession plans	IDP for all direct reports; succession plans at one or more levels below SLT

In the case at hand, we found all business unit directors had strategic plans that met standards, but there was wide variation in the quality and effectiveness of their tactical plans. The star performer developed a number of tactical plans by region, geography, client density, and market segment. Then each tactical plan was tailored across the functional areas of the business unit—sales, marketing, IT, logistics, and operations. The business unit director's role was to ask the question of each functional manager: "What are you doing in this market segment to support the business?"

Case Study: Changing Expectations at a Refinery

In Chapter Five we discussed a star performer found in the control room at a refinery (see Figure 7.2). Not only was he able to keep production within the control limits, but he also kept them at the upper end of production throughout his shift. This translated into significantly higher revenue and profit for the refinery—all while staying within the safe range of production. The typical operators viewed their jobs as simply making sure nothing went wrong as they monitored gauges and alarms, shifted product flows, and adjusted pressures and temperatures. Figuring out how to operate the plant at the higher production levels was something the star operator had already accomplished. We needed to capture his process, document which gauges showed leading indicators, and specify what adjustments he made based on those readings. We then packaged this new procedure into a job aid.

We then obtained management's approval for the revised procedure. Implementing the new procedure with the job aid required management to set new expectations and ensure that coaching feedback was provided to the other operators as they came up to speed with the new approach. Our star operator played a vital role in this stage as well, as he was able to diagnose any missteps on the part of the other operators and to help refine the

Figure 7.2. Control Limit Graph for Petroleum Products

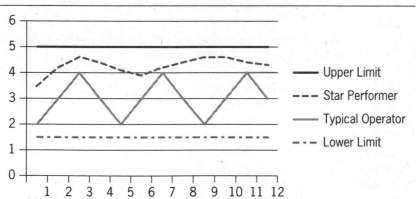

Figure 7.3. Results of Optimized Output

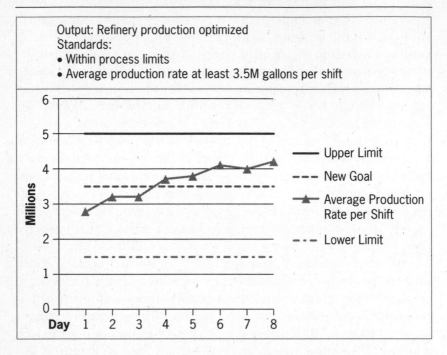

Output: Refinery production optimized
Standards:
• Within process limits
• Average production rate at least 3.5M gallons per shift

job aids that the workers would use. Figure 7.3 shows the results of the workers' progress, which also became part of the feedback mechanism.

Notes

1. Robert J. Rosenthal and Lenora Jacobson, *Pygmalion in the Classroom* (New York: Holt, Rinehart and Winston, 1968).
2. J. Sterling Livingston, *Pygmalion in Management* (Boston: Harvard Business School Publishing Corporation, 2009). Originally published in *Harvard Business Review*, 1969.
3. *Look* Editorial Board, "Sweeney's Miracle," *Look* (November 16, 1965): 117–118.
4. Dov Eden, *Pygmalion in Management: Productivity as a Self-Fulfilling Prophecy* (Lexington, MA: Lexington Books, 1990).x
5. G. Benscoter and E. Guman, "Performance Improvement Success as seen through the cells of the Behavior Engineering Model," in Peter Dean (Ed.), *Performance Engineering at Work* (Batavia, IL: The

International Board of Standards for Training, Performance and Instruction, 1994).

6. William Wiggenhorn, "Motorola U: When Training Becomes an Education," *Harvard Business Review* (July-August 1990).

7. Scott Weiss, "Steve Jobs, Superhero," *TechCrunch*, January 28, 2012, http://techcrunch.com/2012/01/28/steve-jobs-superhero/

8. P. Hersey and K. H. Blanchard, *Management of Organizational Behavior: Utilizing Human Resources*, 3rd ed. (Englewood Cliffs, NJ: Prentice Hall, 1977).

CHAPTER EIGHT

Great Job!

Rewards, Recognition, and Consequences

Figure 8.1. The Role of Rewards, Recognition, and Consequences in the EPS Model

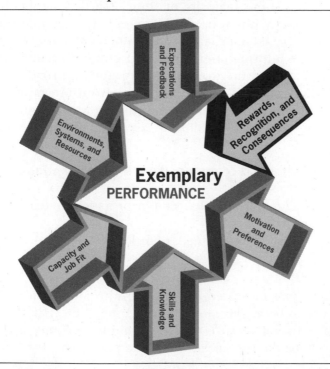

Source: Exemplary Performance, LLC. Copyright 2008–2012.

In This chapter

- Aligning Recognition and Rewards
- Motivators Versus Satisfiers
- Additive Impact and Employee Engagement

Aligning Recognition and Rewards

Figure 8.1 highlights the importance of aligning rewards, recognition, and consequences for poor performance in your organization.

Each branch of the U.S. military has a medals and awards manual that lists criteria and submission procedures for all of the awards for which members in that service branch are eligible. The highest medal is the Congressional Medal of Honor, which is awarded for "conspicuous gallantry and intrepidity at the risk of his or her life above and beyond the call of duty while engaged in an action against an enemy of the United States." From World War II onward, the majority of these awards have been made posthumously.[1] Without doubt, Medals of Honor have significant criteria and are taken seriously. At the other end of the recognition spectrum are informal mementos and praise. Certainly, rewards and recognition in the workplace vary along a broad spectrum. Among the variety of recognition tools you have available, an important consideration is to determine how each can be effectively and aptly used. The following are three important questions to ask:

- Are rewards and recognition aligned with organizational values?
- Are they aligned to the desired performance (of teams and individuals)?
- Are they aligned to the needs of individuals?

What Works?

We believe that most people show up with ample motivation to do a great job on day one (see Chapter Nine). If this is the case, then use of rewards and recognition becomes a confirming activity by the organization for the performance contributed

Rewards and recognition shape the behavior and performance of others as they observe the explicit signals of organizational values.

by individuals and teams. The organizationis saying, "Your performance has provided value to the organization." Through rewards and recognition, the organization demonstrates appreciation in meaningful, tangible ways. Rewards and recognition also shape the behavior and performance of others as they observe the explicit signals of organizational values. It does not have to be complicated, but it does need to be thoughtful.

A case in point comes from our work years ago with the U.S. Postal Service. Following significant technology investment, the Postal Service believed local distribution centers were not embracing the new technology and sorting equipment. Management then put an incentive system in place, providing financial bonuses to center managers for technology utilization. The initial result was that mail was not distributed any faster with the new technology. Closer inspection revealed that managers would actually sort the same mail multiple times per day with the new sorting machines. The technology worked just fine—actually so well that it finished all the day's sorting in about an hour. But because the incentives were based on utilization (how many hours per day the equipment was in use), they would re-sort the mail to drive the utilization metrics up.

Another organization implemented a new bonus system to encourage their sales force to push a new product into their market. The company was surprised when the new bonus initiative had no impact on new product sales. When the company dug a little deeper into why the program was not producing the expected boost in sales, they made a surprising discovery: the *sales force* had quickly figured out they could achieve their bonus level sales numbers more quickly and reliably by continuing to push established product lines and adhering to the existing bonus structure. The learning point is that people tend to be rational!

What Really Motivates and Rewards?

This kind of rational thinking is also a function of the hierarchy of needs espoused by the behavioral psychologist Abraham Maslow.[2]

Some may question certain aspects of his construct, but our purpose is to examine his hierarchy of needs from a practical vantage point. Maslow's general framework is that if your basic physiological needs of food, clothing, shelter, and sex are not met, you are not likely to be focused on meeting higher-level needs such as social contacts, winning the esteem of colleagues, and self-actualizing (Figure 8.2).

We next want to tie in Frederick Herzberg's research about motivators and satisfiers.[3] He concluded that satisfiers (or hygiene factors, as he originally labeled them) are the environmental aspects of the job that connect with lower-level needs. Salary, a safe work environment, job security, supervision, and company policy are factors that, if not met, become sources of job dissatisfaction. However, these are not the factors that cause people to strive to do better; they are not motivators. "The growth or *motivator* factors that are intrinsic to the job are achievement, recognition for achievement, the work itself, responsibility, and growth or advancement."[4]

What we observe in star performers is the ability to make the connection between what they are doing and what they are producing, and to see the connection between what they are producing and how these outputs provide value to the organization.

Figure 8.2. Maslow's Hierarchy of Needs

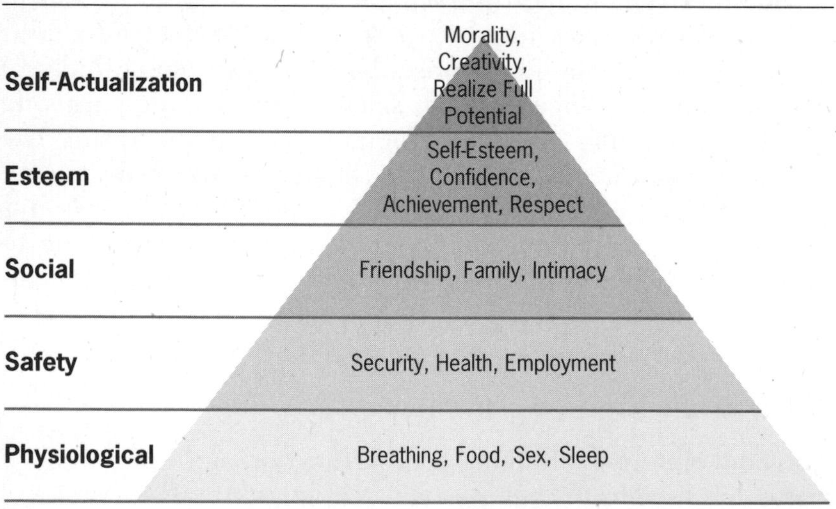

Self-Actualization	Morality, Creativity, Realize Full Potential
Esteem	Self-Esteem, Confidence, Achievement, Respect
Social	Friendship, Family, Intimacy
Safety	Security, Health, Employment
Physiological	Breathing, Food, Sex, Sleep

Moreover, star performers are able to use this value connection as motivation to achieve even greater results. Your job as a manager or leader is to make these connections as visible and real to the rest of the workforce as possible. To do that, effective managers make pathways, recognizing effort and output that are aligned with organizational goals.

Compensation

The principal question to ask about your existing compensation system is whether or not it functions as intended. For purposes of this book, we categorize compensation by three types: recruiting, retention, and results.

- *Recruiting:* Intended to attract competent people to the organization. Is the pay for a particular position set at a market competitive level?
- *Retention:* Set to discourage competent people from leaving the organization. Is there a connection to career advancement?
- *Results:* Intended to link bonuses and pay raises to productivity and thereby encourage competent people to accomplish more. Are significant raises or bonuses tied to superior performance?

In examining a particular compensation system, you should ask whether it is structured in a way that promotes improved performance. For instance, is pay for a particular role considerably lower than for the same job in other organizations? Or do workers feel the value of the job is much higher than the compensation provided? Sometimes the organization is prevented from increasing pay because of law, regulation, union contract, or budget constraints. In such cases, you should ask whether there are benefits that could be added or increased to help overcome or minimize the demotivating impact of perceived lower pay. Some organizations have tight rules that limit pay, but allow for increasing bonuses or other benefits, such as better insurance, better retirement plan contributions, or better working conditions. A key factor in such instances is to ensure that any change in benefits is *relevant* to workers' values.

Compensation Scenarios

Sometimes the negative perception about compensation is within the same organization, where variation in pay exists among workers who have the same job title. This may be for logical reasons: compensation is geared to proficiency levels, by regulation or union contract, or perhaps the higher-paid workers have a higher-valued specialty. When this is the case, managers should communicate not only the reason for the pay differential, but also convey what workers can do to obtain higher pay. For example, learn special skills, produce high-quality outputs, and so on.

A second scenario is when workers expect overtime pay that doesn't happen or when superior performance is not reinforced financially. Although this may be the reality of constrained budgets, you should still find ways to reinforce the actions that the organization values—such as willingness to work overtime and superior performance. Providing for earlier promotion, positive feedback and praise, and recognition through newsletters and public ceremonies may very well be more effective—and viable—than budget-constrained financial rewards.

Types of Recognition

We categorize recognition into three categories:

- *Negative (also called consequences):* Fines for violations of safety practices, reprimands for unacceptable behavior, termination for cause.
- *Sustain or satisfy:* Base pay, fairness in compensation, fairness in work environment.
- *Improve:* Bonuses and benefits as a result of performance. Relevant forms of recognition used to reinforce high performance (based on results and not behavior alone).

Working Conditions

Working conditions can either be a dissatisfier or a motivator. Workload, organizational culture, and type of organization can all function as satisfiers. This means that when "good" they still do not motivate, but all have the potential to be "dissatisfiers" when done poorly or are absent. On the other hand, celebrations, collegiality, choice of projects, esteem of colleagues, and job enrichment can all be motivators. When we examine the world of work today, we find context-specific differences among industries, workers, and functions, and must consider what would be the relevant rewards and recognition for each.

Software Help Desk Example

In one interview with a software help desk person in India, we asked what it was about the job that energized the person. Was it a relatively higher wage than his peers in other industries? "Oh no," he explained, "my pay is about the same as others, but I get to work on the latest technology, the latest and most capable computers." Now this person was not a programmer, but rather a help desk person on the other end of the line whom you call when experiencing problems with your software. The "latest" computer was not really an essential tool for him to perform his work, but this was an important factor of what motivated him in his job.

Refinery Worker Example

The petroleum industry offers opportunity for blue-collar workers to earn significantly higher wages than their counterparts in other industries. Bargaining unit contracts in this industry typically guarantee overtime. This sits in sharp contrast to trends in other industries in which many workers seek employment providing even fewer than 40 hours per week. For the outside operator at an oil refinery, the work can be very cold in winter, very hot in summer, and very dangerous, loud, and bad smelling year-round. Yet there is no shortage of highly capable, willing workers to do this type of work. Why is that? One significant reason is the opportunity to earn a relatively high wage; that is, the rewards are higher. Another is to learn a trade that, in turn, provides employment security.

Do wages alone overcome concerns about safety and a harsh work environment? The company says it cares about worker health and safety. However, the company must demonstrate to workers that its concern is real. One walk around the refinery and you will notice small things. Ample bottled water is always available and free. Earplugs and other safety equipment are always available and provided at no cost to the worker. The people who work at the refinery know it is a dangerous job—but not unnecessarily dangerous. They know there are safeguards in place and that the company follows through with real commitment and not just lip service. Units with unblemished safety records receive catered lunches. The workers know this is not a great expense to the company, but it is still something they appreciate and is aligned with something they care about (their own safety). In summary, this example shows how money or compensation can be a motivator and how lower-level needs, such as safety and health, can be addressed by aligning rewards and recognition.

Motivators Versus Satisfiers

Part of Herzberg's research in workplace motivation involved asking people to describe their most satisfying work experience. From the responses he received, Herzberg identified the following list of motivators. Note that not every motivating factor on the list must be present to increase employee engagement or inspire better performance. Rather, individual workers find their jobs motivating when one or more of these factors are present, relevant, and aligned to their own values:

- Achievement
- Recognition
- Responsibility
- The work itself
- Advancement
- Personal growth

What follows are two examples intended to illuminate how these motivating factors operate in the workplace in different settings.

Pathologist Example

In one project we examined the role of a pathologist for a company that conducts medical testing in laboratory facilities throughout the United States. Pathologists are first educated and trained as physicians and then complete their residency specializing in the cause and development of disease. Because this company has facilities across the United States, one of the ways to provide recognition is to publish stories in its company magazine and regional newsletters.

Publishing this story in the company magazine and elsewhere had a tremendously positive impact on others throughout the company.

None of the pathologists interviewed said they wished they could work overtime to earn more money. What did appeal to them was the opportunity to attend professional conferences and make presentations about their research (that is, recognition of their achievements was motivating).

One story was about how the company had won a contract with a European government with socialized medicine. The country had a backlog of PAP tests in which the turnaround time to provide results to patients reached as high as nine months. After six months of taking on this work, the backlog of 50,000 PAP smears had been cleared and turnaround time was down to one month. By the end of the first year, the time was down to two weeks and they were testing 300,000 PAP smears for this client per year. To put this in greater context, one of the primary uses of PAP smears is to test for cervical cancer, which is the third leading cause of cancer deaths in women worldwide. Two years before this initiative, 200 women in this European country were diagnosed with cervical cancer and of these, more than 90 died. Such a high mortality rate is due in part to delays in diagnosis and treatment.

Of course, there were people in roles other than pathologists who contributed to this achievement. But the story was a great victory for women's health and was accomplished by the combined efforts of two of the company's facilities. Publishing this story in the company magazine and elsewhere provided recognition to those directly involved and had a tremendously positive impact on others throughout the company.

IT Manager Example

Kathy was an IT manager in a 40,000-person organization and had been selected for one of the top national leadership awards. The selection was not only for the leadership traits she demonstrated, but also for the results she had achieved. When asked for some nuggets about how she achieved such results, she said she finds reasons to celebrate with her people and goes about it with intentionality. She will bring 40 people together, buy a cake for someone's birthday, highlight milestones that people have completed on major projects, and even draw attention to significant achievements in personal development (such as college degrees earned through part-time study). This was affirmed in our observations; her people are involved in information technology and most work alone or in small teams and rarely get direct feedback from the end users. However, we readily observed the high spirits and satisfaction that these frequent, informal recognition and celebration events produced.

Role of Clear Expectations

Rewards, recognition, and incentives are most effective when closely entwined with clear expectations and feedback. Specifically, this is how we approach these concepts in our work:

- Expectations and feedback are specific to the work being performed and the criteria around how the outputs of that work are evaluated.
- Rewards, recognition, and incentives are explicitly about making and reinforcing the linkages between performance and the value produced.

As demonstrated in the short examples in this chapter and characterized by the common lament about organizations "rewarding the wrong things," achieving alignment among performance influences is essential for an Exemplary Performance System.

As is the case with feedback, you should also be concerned with frequency and timeliness when designing recognition and rewards. If we hope to shape behavior and, by extension, to improve performance, the linkages between performance and reward must be clear. In the classic 1989 comedy, *Christmas Vacation*, the bumbling character Clark Griswald (portrayed by Chevy Chase) opens an envelope that contains his annual Christmas bonus, having just proclaimed that if it's what he thinks it is, he is putting in a new family swimming pool. To his dismay, his envelope contains a membership in the "Jelly of the Month Club." Similar to this workplace parody, how many employees in the real world see no relationship between their efforts and accomplishments and the bonuses they receive? Or the time delay is so great between superior performance and recognition that the recognition has no impact?

Timeliness of Recognition

There are also examples of good intentions gone awry. The federal government has a program for "on-the-spot" cash awards. The cynicism among some employees is that the $100 cash awards have had a negative impact on a person's take-home pay after taxes (if they had been on the fringe of the next tax bracket). The other quandary is that "on-the-spot" really wasn't—because the actual money would show up in the recipient's pay two to four weeks later. Or military awards are delayed in processing and thus mailed to the service member's next duty station. To service members

How many employees see no relationship between their efforts and accomplishments and the bonuses they receive?

who departed units anticipating this form of recognition, these are bad experiences, communicating that the organization does not really value their efforts and accomplishments. When workers perceive disparity or unfairness in rewards and recognition, the experience is a negative one.

On the other hand, a rational system provides recognition as a function of the value produced by employee outputs. We have seen great examples in which bonuses and compensation were tied to multiple outputs and proportionally weighted by value contribution to the organization. For recognition purposes, our example of IT manager Kathy finding reasons to "celebrate" informally is spot-on for closing the gap between valued performance and timely recognition. A good explanation along with attendant organizational results comes from Grand Master Haeng Ung Lee, 9th degree black belt and founder of the American Taekwondo Association (ATA), currently the largest martial arts organization in the United States. He recalls that when he was a student of Taekwondo in the 1950s, there were only three "color" belts: white, green, and brown. The levels from beginner to black belt count down, with 9th grade being the beginner white belt. (Black belt levels are denoted by "degrees" rather than "grades" and count up from 1st degree black belt to 9th degree black belt.) Lee writes that when he moved from 9th grade up to 6th grade, he still wore the white belt and that there was no visible recognition of the achievement. When he founded the ATA in 1969, they had the same number of grades (nine), but had increased the number of color belts (see Table 8.1). Lee subsequently went on to establish a different color belt with each grade. He explained that the purpose was not to increase the time it took to attain black belt, but rather to provide more frequent *visible recognition* of the progress that students were making.[5] From its humble beginnings in an Omaha, Nebraska, YMCA in 1969, the ATA now has over 300,000 students and 1,500 schools in North America.

Table 8.1. Color Belts of the American Taekwondo Association

Grade	1950	1970	Current Day
9th	White	White	White
8th	White	White	Orange
7th	White	Yellow	Yellow
6th	White	Yellow	Camouflage
5th	Green	Green	Green
4th	Green	Green	Purple
3rd	Green	Blue	Blue
2nd	Green	Blue	Brown
1st	Brown	Red	Red

Culturally Relevant Recognition

Margo Murray, writing about mentoring programs, points out that one of the most commonly mentioned obstacles to structuring the mentoring process is when there is no perceived reward, benefit, or payoff for the mentor.[6] One of the motivators previously mentioned was recognition through job title. Murray cautions that in facilitated mentoring programs, choosing a title for the person in the role of mentor is dependent on the organizational culture.

"Some organizations are comfortable with the term mentor, while others think it is too trendy for their own programs. The term must be one that most people in the organization can be comfortable with, particularly the mentors themselves."[7] She suggests alternative titles such as "coach" or "exemplar." The point is to ensure that you select types of recognition (even titles) that are relevant to the culture of the organization.

> *Ensure that you select types of recognition (even titles) that are relevant to the culture of the organization.*

We know of a variety of types of recognition and celebration rewards that are treasured in some organizations, but would be absurd in others. YUM! Brands has a book for internal use with all kinds of examples of low-cost/no-cost recognition, including having a group of coworkers march over to a recognized person's cubical all playing kazoos! Gostick and Elton mention a purple water buffalo statue in the executive office at Madison Square Garden to denote exceptional effort, and in another organization they highlight an old bowling trophy, spray-painted orange. It has become a form of recognition passed around every few days to teammates who demonstrate a value that moves the team closer to its goals.[8]

At Agilent's high-tech repair and calibration facilities, visibly recognizing technical depth was identified as a powerful strategy for reinforcing the type of expertise that brought value to the organization. The solution for underscoring this expertise was appliqués on lab coats that denoted levels of technical depth. The common thread in these examples is to link activity and accomplishment to organizational goals—and then celebrate and recognize people with rewards that are *relevant* to them and *fit the organizational culture*.

Some Contrarian Views

Why should people be rewarded for just doing their jobs? Such a statement is more of a reflection of perceived inequities in the rewards and recognition systems of the organization than an argument against rewards or recognition. If people are engaging in activities that produce outputs of value to the organization, then "just doing their job" is, in fact, providing value to the organization and should be recognized! Sometimes such sentiments are a perceived slight in proportion: one person makes valued contributions over the course of the year and receives the same reward or recognition that someone else accrues from a short-term but highly visible project. One could certainly argue whether equal contributions were being equally rewarded. Rewarding effort is only appropriate when we have clarity that the effort is aligned to the right outputs. We met a team that put in long hours and tremendous effort each year producing an annual report. The previous CEO had left four years earlier and had been the last person to read this type of annual report!

Additive Impact and Employee Engagement

Dr. Dale Brethower, professor of psychology at Western Michigan University, compiled research showing productivity gains (see Table 8.2) from the additive effects of aligning expectations, feedback, rewards, and recognition.[9]

The first two initiatives in the table are actions that we covered in Chapter Seven: provide clear expectations about what should be produced along with standards and criteria around those job outputs. We also suggest providing feedback in a graphical manner (if possible) so that workers can readily identify progress. The third initiative is about reinforcing production of those results with praise and recognition in a nonmonetary manner. The fourth initiative—adding a pay-for-performance system—provides confidence that the incentivized performance is the right performance that drives organizational results in measurable ways.

Table 8.2. Additive Productivity Gains from Expectations, Feedback, Rewards, and Recognition

Item	Initiative	Result in Productivity
1	Installing a good work measurement system where none exists or replacing a not-so-good work measurement system.	10%+ improvement
2	With a good work measurement system in place, installing an objective feedback system to supplement it.	15%+ improvement
3	With a good feedback system in place, installing nonmonetary incentive systems.	15%+ improvement
4	With a nonmonetary incentive system in place (based on good work measurement and objective feedback), installing a monetary pay-for-performance system.	10%+ improvement

Employee Engagement

Definitions of employee engagement vary by organization and among those advocating particular interventions (Figure 8.3). Clearly there is overlap among the ingredients of employee engagement, Herzberg's motivators, and elements of the EPS Model. Where employee engagement is measured, but no actions taken as a result, employee engagement goes down. Although

Figure 8.3. Dilbert on Employee Engagement

some organizational experts advocate that employee satisfaction scores are a true measure of employee engagement, this is really a lagging indicator of how well the business is running. Establishing an effective recognition system is a driver for both employee engagement and a leading indicator of high business performance. The essential elements for creating or improving employee engagement and improving business results comes about in workplaces that are intentional about the following:

- Status: job title and perception of importance;
- Clarity of expectations for work and resources to accomplish the work (tools, equipment);
- Advancement or career opportunities;
- Regular feedback;
- Quality of relationships with peers, superiors, and subordinates;
- Perception of organizational values; and
- Reward or incentives for good work.

In concert with the research firm Best Companies Group, Gostick and Elton examined Best Places to Work data and concluded that in organizations that made the Best List, 84% of employees felt they received enough recognition for work that is well done. In companies who did not make the Best Places to Work list, only 69% of employees reported feeling the same about recognition. It is interesting to note that the companies in this research are a biased sample, in that they were companies that already believed they were competitive enough to make the Best Places to Work and had invited the examination by researchers.[10]

> *Recognition divides "good" from "great" teams.*

Gostick and Elton consider recognition an "accelerant" to what they term the Basic 4 of the best managers: goal setting, communication, trust, and accountability.[11] Furthermore, in their research of the best managers—those who achieve enhanced business results—recognition divides "good" from "great" teams. In fact, getting teams to cheer one another, independent of the manager or leader, is a tremendous plus. Making this a group norm is possible once clarity is established about what good work looks like—that is, work that contributes and provides value to the organizational goals.

Availability

This almost goes without saying, but it is impossible to have a vibrant recognition system if the manager is not accessible. Companies that seek to be innovative and fresh require a culture that allows challenges to the status quo. Developing that culture—or helping a workforce change from where it is today to where the organization wants to go—comes by way of encouraging, recognizing, and rewarding the new behavior. To reward it, you must first recognize it. To recognize it, you have to be able to observe by making yourself available.

Consequences

Newton's third law of motion says that for every action there is an equal and opposite reaction. We tend to think that human interactions are not subject to the laws of physics. However, for every action in a workplace there are consequences. These consequences fall into one of three categories; management can:

- Reward: through praise, recognition, or reward
- Punish: with some negative result (from reprimand, to a harsh look, to corrective feedback)
- Ignore

We find the third category especially problematic. Behavioral psychology tells us that behaviors that are not reinforced will eventually fade away. If we ask for ideas and innovations and never act upon those ideas, nor reward the activity, then employee enthusiasm to provide ideas will eventually disappear. If team members are being disruptive and never receive corrective feedback, then this behavior will eventually fade away. However, hoping that non-value-producing behavior fades sooner, rather than later, is not an effective strategy.

Summary

Valued activity is reinforced and accelerated by recognition and reward—affirming to the performer and others in the organization that his or her contribution was noticed and valuable.

The best managers provide clear expectations up front, along with confirming feedback shortly after the production of the valuable output. This valued activity is reinforced and accelerated by recognition and reward—affirming to the performer and others in the organization that his or her contribution was noticed and valuable. Taken together, then, these elements have an especially powerful additive effect. When begun with alignment to organizational goals through the work outputs that people produce on the job, recognition and reward systems are powerful levers for driving business results. The next chapter discusses how internal motivation, passion, and intentionality on the part of the performer contribute to exemplary performance and how each of us can accelerate our own potential into greater results.

Notes

1. U.S. Army Military History website, compiled from the archives of the Congressional Medal of Honor Society, 40 Patriots Point Rd., Mt. Pleasant, SC 29464. http://www.history.army.mil/html/moh/mohstats.html.
2. Abraham Maslow, *Motivation and Personality* (New York: Harper, 1954).
3. F. I. Herzberg, "One More Time: How Do You Motivate Employees?" *Harvard Business Review*, 65, no. 5 (Sep/Oct, 1987): 109–120.
4. Ibid.
5. H. U. Lee, *The Way of Traditional Taekwondo. Volume A: Philosophy and Traditions* (Little Rock, AR: ATA Publications, 1993).
6. Margo Murray, *Beyond the Myths and Magic of Mentoring* (San Francisco: Jossey-Bass, 1991), 59.
7. Ibid., 114.
8. A. Gostick and C. Elton, *The Orange Revolution* (New York: Free Press, 2010).
9. Dale Brethower, "Strategic Improvement of Workplace Competence II: The Economics of Competence," *Performance Improvement Quarterly*, 6, no. 2 (1993).
10. Gostick and Elton, *The Orange Revolution*.
11. Ibid.

CHAPTER NINE

How to Succeed in Business by Really Trying

Motivation, Intentionality, and Deliberate Practice

Figure 9.1. The Role of Motivation and Preferences in the EPS Model

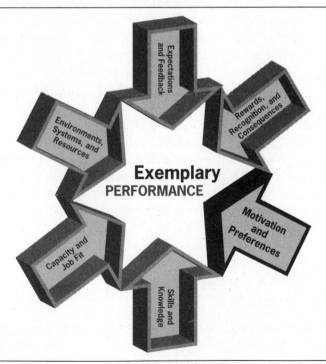

Source: Exemplary Performance, LLC. Copyright 2008–2012.

In This chapter

- Motivation
- Key Parts of a Motivational System
- Intentionality
- Deliberate Practice

Motivation

Exceptionally high performers exhibit a level of drive that separates them from those who are simply solid, strong performers
(Figure 9.1). As we noted in Chapter Five, these exemplars strive
to excel and improve over time. They work tirelessly to exceed
the levels of all other performers and work diligently to stay at
the top of their game. Not surprisingly, these individuals are often
prominently successful, not only inside their organizations, but in
the society at large.

Michael Oher, an offensive lineman for the NFL's Baltimore
Ravens, is a good example of a motivated star performer. You
might know the six-foot-four player's name because you just
happen to be a sports fan, or you might have read his 2010
autobiography, *I Beat the Odds*, which chronicles how he escaped
the slums of Memphis to become a star in the NFL. Perhaps a
more familiar cue might be the 2009 movie *The Blind Side*, starring
Sandra Bullock as Leigh Anne Tuohy, Michael's adoptive mother. Tuohy was a
well-heeled Memphis suburbanite who pushed the awkward, struggling adoles-
cent to succeed in the classroom and on the football field.

Exemplary performers appear to sustain their internal motivation in spite of the other barriers within the organization's work systems.

While acknowledging the extraordinary luck and impact of having a
strong-willed adoptive mother who refused to take no for an
answer, Michael's autobiography stresses his strong motivation to
overcome his past. He writes:

> When I was drafted in the first round by the Baltimore Ravens,
> I knew I had done the impossible. I hadn't just beaten the odds;

I had blown them out of the water. But the story isn't just about arriving at the pros. My goal had never been just to get the offer, or to sign the contract, or to get the paycheck. I wanted to *do* something, to know that I was working each day to do something with my potential, pushing myself to make sure that I was always giving my all. Making it to the pros wasn't the finish line for me. The world is full of people who get their big shot and then never did anything with it.[1]

Motivation, we would argue, is something that we all bring to the job, at least initially. If you think back to your first day on a job, you probably got up early, obsessed over what to wear, showed up early, and likely had a little bounce in your step brought on by thoughts of all the ways you planned to succeed in your new job. Perhaps you, like Michael Oher, are one of the fortunate individuals who have managed to maintain that positive spring in your step months or even years later. Congratulations, for you are indeed blessed.

> *"I wanted to do something, to know that I was working each day to do something with my potential, pushing myself to make sure that I was always giving my all."*
>
> —Michael Oher

However, most are not so fortunate. Usually it takes only six months for the ineffective systems and broken processes found in most organizations to wipe out these positive expectations about what an individual performer can achieve. So what happened? Did these hopeful, positive new hires just run out of steam and lose their motivation to do a good job? Or is there something else going on? Perhaps there's something terribly wrong with the "work environment" that is sucking the motivational life out of these once bright-eyed employees. To continue optimal performance, a leader must provide a systematic motivational design that aligns with the needs of each performer or team.

Key Parts of a Motivational System

A motivational system consists of:

- The individual and his or her particular set of internal motivational characteristics, which include a person's internal curiosity, motives, and expectations of success, and

- The work environment and the tactics and strategies that affect the goal-directed efforts and responses of individuals to the system. These factors include job complexity, leadership style, and job fit.

Within the motivational system are the performance impacts that occur after a task has been carried out, that is, the personal satisfaction or dissatisfaction which ultimately influences our desire to continue pursuing the same or similar goals. Satisfaction is also influenced by the feedback obtained, the rewards given, and by an individual's perception of overall fairness.

External Influences

We often assume that the individual performer is responsible for providing the internal motivation needed to excel at a job. "Can't find the passion to succeed? Then find a job that will ignite and inspire your lagging motivational spirit." However, changing jobs is not always the answer, nor is it always the most effective path to high performance. A more satisfactory path in many cases is the intervention of an effective leader who inspires motivation through positive modeling and by encouraging positive individual behaviors via feedback.

> The goal of a motivational system is to enable optimal levels of performance, not simply to provide comfort, pleasure, or entertainment.

Motivation is a means, not an end. The goal of a motivational system is to enable optimal levels of performance, not simply to provide comfort, pleasure, or entertainment. A well-designed motivational system allows workers who are willing and able to accept the requirements to perform at targeted levels, while at the same time feeling challenged, effective, important, and satisfied.

Systematic design and implementation offers a way to influence motivation in a predictable and measurable way. It is the leader's job to ensure the implementation of effective and operational motivational systems that enable and support exceptional performance.

Four Key Motivation Components

In the abstract, motivation might seem a fairly straightforward problem to tackle, yet research has shown that the mechanics are quite complex. Following are four key components of human motivation—attention, relevance, confidence, and satisfaction—that research has identified:[2]

1. *Attention:* People need stimulation and variety, although the level of stimulation everyone craves is not the same. Some people have high levels of sensation-seeking behavior, whereas others prefer a more peaceful and predictable environment. So when selecting workers for a job, it is important to match them to a position with an appropriate level of stimulation. When a perfect match is not possible, a second strategy is to provide access to job-enrichment programs to enhance the quantity and complexity of a job's baseline requirements.

2. *Relevance:* People need to understand the "worth of their work" or, more plainly stated, "why" they are performing a particular job. An individual's perception of relevance depends on a match between his or her motives and values, the job design, and the culture of the organization. For example, high achievers prefer clearly defined goals and take personal responsibility for their success. These individuals also need frequent feedback on their progress toward goals, access to experts if they need help, and control over the resources necessary to accomplish a task. In contrast, people with a high need for affiliation enjoy working in groups and building close relationships with others.

   Relevance is encouraged through healthy competition and encouraging win-win cooperation. Competition is an ingrained part of the human condition, so depending on how you use it, competitive activities can either enhance productivity or be a divisive tool that harms or diminishes productivity. Motivation and performance are increased when people work in a cooperative environment toward common goals and receive incentives for outstanding personal accomplishment.

3. *Confidence:* Performance is also increased when performers feel competent and in control. For example, workers are able to tolerate a higher level of stress without ill effect if they

believe they have some measure of control over what happens to them. In addition, self-esteem increases if workers are able to make decisions regarding both the type of work and their approach to the work they do. Consequently, any motivational component of a performance system design must include mechanisms that make it possible for performers to feel this sense of control. The benefits of such a design include more healthy and productive behaviors, as well as increased worker confidence.

4. *Satisfaction:* Well-designed performance systems should include ample opportunities for workers to feel good about themselves and their accomplishments. These good feelings can come from extrinsic rewards such as money, but financial compensation is not always effective or even possible.

Fortunately, other powerful yet effective and inexpensive incentives exist that can be used to bolster any motivational system, including positive social recognition for the valued efforts and accomplishments of a contributor. This is especially true when this recognition comes from peers and superiors.

Intentionality

As we pointed out in Chapter Five, the most reliable way to create clarity of expectation is by focusing on the desired output and the corresponding metrics. Exemplary performers, as we noted in that chapter, tend to focus on accomplishments (results, outputs, or deliverables) rather than on activities or tasks. This focus provides them with a clear picture of their goals and helps them accurately judge whether or not they are producing worthy accomplishments.

> *People perform at a consistently higher level when they understand the worth of their work.*

To illustrate this point is a story from twelfth-century Paris. A man was walking along the Seine and came upon a large construction site. He stopped and asked a mason what he was doing and the response was, "I'm laying stone." Several meters later the man asked another mason the same question. This time the response was, "I'm building a wall." Finally, after several minutes, the man again asked the question of a third mason whose work quality was exceptional. This time the response was, "I'm building a great cathedral to the glory of God."

Whether or not this story about three masons working on the Notre Dame Cathedral is true, our experience tells us that the point it makes is valid; people perform at a consistently higher level when they understand the worth of their work. It's easy to see the performance difference between someone focused on simply completing activities (laying one more stone) and someone who understands the value of his or her contribution—someone focused on producing an accomplishment that matters, such as the Cathedral of Notre Dame.

An added value to having clarity around accomplishments is the elimination of non-value-added activity. Exemplary performers quickly adjust their performance when they realize an activity is not leading to the desired result. Michael Oher, mentioned at the beginning of this chapter, offers some lessons here when he described how he was focused on maintaining the starting player position.

> That's really my goal—to be the hardest working guy in the NFL. My conditioning coaches sometimes tease me because I am so stubborn about getting in my workouts. I never, ever miss a practice, never miss a training session. Some of my friends think it's funny that I'm working on flexibility with the goal of doing a full split. I know guys my size don't really seem like the bendy gymnast type, but I've heard that there are one or two tackles out there on the other teams who can do the splits, so that's become one of my motivations: if they can do it, I should be able to, too. It's about always looking forward and making sure that you give your job all that you've got. If I lose my starting position, it had better be because there was someone out there with more talent, not because I just didn't push myself enough.[3]

The leader's role in supporting the intentionality of his or her team should include the following strategies and focus:

- Provide clarity in how your team's accomplishments fit into the organization as a whole—that is, a clear definition of the team's value proposition. Consider what the impact is, both upstream and downstream, when expectations are missed, met, or exceeded.

- Ensure that each team member has clarity around his or her accomplishments—what the outputs should be, when they are due, and how he or she will be judged.
- Provide frequent, targeted feedback on progress to both team and individual performers.
- Give specific corrective feedback (quantity, quality, timeliness) when a performer or team's accomplishments are inadequate.

Practicing these leadership behaviors will support, sustain, and enhance the intentionality that your team members bring to the table.

Deliberate Practice

As discussed in Chapter Five, many have heard about the research that shows mastery is the result of at least 10,000 hours of practice (about five years of 40 hours of practice per week). And yet we know that few people are truly great at what they do, even after five years of experience. But why aren't they? Why don't they manage businesses like Jack Welch or play golf like Tiger Woods?

Asked to explain why a few people truly excel, most of us offer one of two answers. The first is *hard work*. Yet hard workers aren't always great performers. The other possibility is that exemplary performers possess an *innate talent* for excelling in their field. The trouble is, scientific evidence doesn't support the notion that specific natural talents make great performers.

So what's the real solution to the mystery of high performance? According to author Geoff Colvin, both the hard work and natural talent camps are wrong. Colvin says in his 2008 book, *Talent Is Overrated,* that what really makes the difference is a highly specific kind of effort called "deliberate practice."[4] Based on extensive research cited in the book, Colvin debunks the myth that innate talent alone is sufficient for success. He shows that great performance is not something reserved for a preordained few, and although the price may be high, it is available to us all.

As we noted in Chapter Five, renowned gold medal champion Michael Phelps practices six hours a day, six days a week, and swims close to fifty miles every week. However, this focused, deliberate practice is quite different from simply showing up for work for 10,000 hours over five years. To this point, an updated version of the old saying "practice makes perfect" is in order. More accurately, the statement should be "practice makes permanent, but only perfect practice makes perfect."

> *Great performance is not something reserved for a preordained few, and although the price may be high, it is available to us all.*

The attainment of expertise in business requires more than talent, initial interest, and high-quality coaching. Successful performers need personal initiative, diligence, and especially a high quantity and quality of practice in order to maintain high levels of performance. Regarding quality, the practice of experts is characterized by its conscious, deliberate properties—namely a high level of concentration and the structuring of specific practice tasks tied to appropriate personal goals, feedback, and opportunities for repetition and error correction. In addition, strategic awareness (a high level of personal awareness) is necessary to overcome existing patterns so that the performer is able to accurately self-monitor and make required adjustments or improvements. For example, in an educational setting, a skilled teacher may provide classroom instruction and practice assignments as homework, but in the end, the aspiring expert (the student) must take the initiative toward becoming an expert on his or her own.

K. Anders Ericsson describes a person's attempts to acquire expertise as deliberate problem solving because it includes three elements: forming a cognitive representation of both the accomplishment and the task, choosing an appropriate technique or strategy, and self-evaluation and correction.[5] These properties of deliberate practice have been studied as key components of self-regulation, where self-regulation is defined as self-generated thoughts, feelings, and actions that are strategically planned and adapted for the attainment of personal goals.

The odds are that few, if any, of the people around you are truly great at what they do—and by great we mean world-class stars. And the hard truth is that very few of the workers around you will ever achieve this level of excellence. It's not a reality most of us focus on, but understanding the reasons behind this "excellence gap" is critically important to the success or failure of organizations, the causes we believe in, and even the lives we lead.

Extensive research in a wide range of fields, such as accounting, medicine, equipment repair, and plant operations, demonstrates that most people not only fail to reach "outstanding" status, but even worse, they frequently don't get any better at their jobs, even after years of experience.

Understanding the exact source of extraordinary performance is crucial, because this knowledge helps identify what *does not* drive high performance in organizations. It is also this knowledge that provides the first step toward discovering what in fact *does* drive and support extraordinary performance.

If it turns out that we're all wrong about talent, that's a big problem. Our views about talent, which are extremely deeply held, are extraordinarily important for the future of our lives, our children's lives, our companies, and the people in them. Understanding the truth about talent is worth a great deal. A number of researchers now argue that giftedness or talent means nothing like what we think it means, if indeed it means anything at all. When researchers have looked at large numbers of high achievers, at least in certain fields, most of the people who became extremely good in their fields did not show early evidence of being gifted. No specific genes identifying particular talents have been found. The most one can say is that if genes exert any influence, then they contribute far less than other factors that support the achievement of the highest levels of performance.

Earlier in his career, researchers on great performance some-times called Tiger Woods the Mozart of golf, and the parallels do seem striking. Here's the situation: Tiger was born into the home of an expert golfer and self-confessed "golf addict." Tiger's father, Earl, was a teacher with a lifelong passion for sports. Earl loved to teach and was eager to begin teaching his new son to golf as soon as possible. Earl gave Tiger his first metal club, a putter, at the age of seven months. Before Tiger was two, they were at the golf course playing and practicing regularly.

Neither Tiger nor his father suggested that Tiger came into this world with a gift for golf. Tiger has repeatedly credited his father for his success. Asked to explain Tiger's phenomenal success, both father and son always gave the same reason: hard work.

In Search of Business Talent

The overwhelming impression that comes from examining the early lives of business stars is that they didn't seem to exhibit any identifiable gift or give any early indication of what they would become. As an example, Jack Welch showed no particular inclination toward business leadership during his early career. He majored not in business or economics, but in chemical engineering, and earned a master's and a PhD in that field. At age 25, he decided to accept an offer to work in a chemical development operation at General Electric. If there was anything in Welch's history to suggest that he would become the most influential business manager of his time, it's tough—in fact, impossible—to spot it.

In surveying the world's business titans, we find many Welch-like stories. These leaders often lacked even a hint of special talent toward the fields that would one day lead to fame and riches. For most of us, the critical point is that, at the very least, innate talents are much less important than we usually think. They seem not to play the crucial role that we generally assign to them, and it's far from clear what role they do play.

Everywhere we see successful companies apparently filled with people who exhibit exceptional talent or potential. So it's definitely surprising to find that research doesn't support the view that extraordinary natural abilities are necessary for high achievement. A wide range of research shows that the correlations between IQ and achievement aren't nearly as strong as we have been led to believe and that, in many cases, there's no correlation at all. In fact, in a wide range of fields, including business, the connection between general intelligence and specific abilities is weak.

The evidence is similar when it comes to that "other general ability" we often associate with extraordinarily successful people—an amazing memory. A large mass of recent evidence shows that memory ability is acquired, and it can be acquired by pretty much anyone. The widespread view that highly accomplished people have tremendous memories is, in one sense, justified. They often astound us with what they can remember! But the view that their amazing ability is a rare natural gift is not justified. Remarkable memory ability is apparently available to anyone.

It may seem surprising that off-the-chart general abilities, especially intelligence and memory, are not necessary for extraordinary achievement, but it becomes less surprising when we consider the qualities that highly successful companies and business leaders look for in employees. It's striking to notice the companies that don't put extreme cognitive abilities at the top of the list—or sometimes even on the list. The message from these companies raises an important question: Even if superior intelligence and memory aren't the critical factors for success, are the traits the companies seek—team orientation, humor, confidence, and so on—reliably related to success across companies? And if so, are they innate traits that you either have or you don't?

What's also surprising is that when it comes to innate, unalterable limits on what healthy adults can achieve, anything beyond basic physical constraints is in dispute. That fact is profoundly opposed to what most of us believe. We tend to think that we are forever barred from all manner of successes because of what we were or were not born with. But what we'd really like to know is not what does or doesn't stop us, but *what makes some people go so much further than others?* And what we have discovered so far is not what makes some people excel, but rather what doesn't. Specifically:

- It isn't experience.
- It isn't specific inborn abilities.
- It isn't general abilities, such as intelligence and memory.

In short, we've nailed down what doesn't drive great performance. So what does? Deliberate practice makes all the difference. Or, as it was stated recently with stark clarity: "The differences between expert performers and normal adults reflect a lifelong period of deliberate effort to improve performance in a specific domain." This is highly significant for two reasons. First, it explicitly rejects the "you've got it or you don't" view. Second, it resolves the huge contradiction in the body of scholarly research on performance and high achievement, as well as our everyday experience. On the one hand, we see everywhere that years of hard work do not make most people great at what they do. On the other hand, we see repeatedly that the people who have achieved the most are the ones who have worked the hardest. How can both sets of observations be true?

The problem, observed the researchers, is that the current definition of practice is unclear. Their framework is based on the highly specific concept of deliberate practice. Precisely what this means turns out to be critically important. An understanding of it illuminates the path to high achievement in *any* field, not just by individuals, but also by teams and organizations. Deliberate practice isn't work and it isn't play; it is something entirely unto itself. What we think of as practice frequently isn't what the researchers mean by deliberate practice. Deliberate practice is characterized by several elements, each worth examining. It is activity designed specifically to improve performance, often with a coach's help; it can be repeated a lot; feedback on results is continuously available; it's highly demanding mentally (whether the activity is purely intellectual or heavily physical); and it isn't much fun.

What we generally do at work is directly opposed to the first principle: it isn't designed by anyone to make us better at anything. Usually, it isn't designed at all; we're just given an objective that's necessary to meet the employer's goals and are expected to get on with it. As for the second principle, the activities that would make us better are usually not highly repeatable. Even in jobs where we do the same few things, we face few incentives to get better at them by exceeding our limits and discovering what we can't do well. Feedback? At most companies this is a travesty, consisting of occasional performance reviews, dreaded by the person delivering them and the one receiving them. Work is often not fun, because accomplishing anything in the real world is a grind. If that's life in most companies, then the opportunities for achieving advantage by adopting the principles of great

The opportunities for achieving advantage by adopting the principles of great performance within organizations would seem to be huge—and they are!

performance within organizations would seem to be huge—and they are!

Deliberate practice does not fully explain high achievement—real life is too complicated for that. A person's circumstances, especially in childhood, can powerfully affect his or her opportunities to engage in deliberate practice. It turns out that deliberate practice can extend one's ability to perform at higher levels far longer than most people believe. In addition, even though performance seems to improve with increased deliberate practice in a wide range of research studies, it must also be true that the relationship cannot be simple and direct in every case. Regardless of how well practice is designed, another important variable is how much effort a person puts into it. When we see great performers doing what they do, it frequently strikes us that they've practiced for so long, and done it so many times, that they can just do it automatically. But in fact, what they have achieved is the ability to avoid doing it automatically. Exemplary performers never allow themselves to reach the automatic, arrested development stage in their chosen fields. The essence of practice, which is continually trying to do the things one cannot do comfortably, makes automatic behavior impossible. Ultimately, the performance is always conscious and controlled, far from automatic.

What makes deliberate practice work? It turns out the answer is the same, whether we look at business or sports or any other field, and it isn't what you might expect. The most important effect of practice in great performers is that it takes them around the limitations that most of us think of as barriers. It enables them to perceive more, to know more, and to remember more than most people.

Top performers can figure out what's going to happen sooner than average performers by *seeing more*. Sometimes excellent performers see more by developing a better and faster understanding of what they see. The superior perceptions of top performers extend beyond the sense of sight. They hear more when they listen and feel more when they touch. When excellent performers look further ahead than average performers do, they are literally looking into their own future. Anticipating what lies ahead for them, they prepare for it and thus perform better. They may be looking only one second ahead, but for them that extra moment makes all the difference. Much of the power of looking further ahead comes from the simple act of raising one's gaze and getting a new perspective, and doing it not once or occasionally, but using practice principles to do it often and become better at it.

Top performers in a wide range of fields have better organized and consolidated knowledge, forming rich mental models of their expertise. This enables them to approach problems in fundamentally different and more effective ways. Many of the best-performing companies explicitly recognize the importance of deep knowledge in their domains, as opposed to general managerial ability. Building and developing knowledge is one of the things that deliberate practice accomplishes. Always trying to extend one's abilities in a field requires amassing additional knowledge and staying at it for years, developing the critical connections to organize all that knowledge and make it useful.

Top performers understand their field at a higher level than average performers do and have a superior structure for remembering information about it. Practice can actually alter the physical nature of a person's brain and body. Endurance runners have larger than average hearts, an attribute that most of us see as one of the natural advantages with which they were blessed. But research has shown that their hearts grow after years of intensive training.

Applying These Principles in Our Lives

To begin applying these principles of deliberate practice in our lives, we must be clear about what we want to accomplish. The requirements for achieving exceptional performance are so great, and take so many years, that no one has a chance of meeting them without deep, consistent commitment. From this perspective, we can see mentors in a new way—not just as wise people to whom we turn for guidance, but as experienced masters in our field who can advise us on the skills and abilities we need to acquire and who can provide feedback on how we're doing. The skills and abilities we can choose to develop are infinite, but the opportunities to practice them fall into two general categories: opportunities to practice in simulated environments and opportunities to practice as part of the work itself.

Many important elements of business life can be practiced. One of the most dreaded tasks for many managers is giving job evaluations to their direct reports. The message can be broken down into pieces and each piece analyzed for intent, then practiced repeatedly with immediate feedback from a coach or by video.

The case method has been used widely in business education for 80 years. You're presented with a problem, and your job is to figure out a solution. The process of focusing on the problem and evaluating proposed solutions is a powerful form of deliberate practice.

The practice of top athletes falls into two large categories. One is conditioning and the other is working on specific critical skills. As an example of developing specific critical skills, in a recent interview with David Letterman, Larry Bird stated that at the height of his career he would shoot 700 or more jump shots every day.

In a business setting, conditioning means getting stronger with the analytical skills you already have, thus enhancing the fundamental skills that underlie your work. Specific skill development is based on focused simulation, and this concept can be applied widely in business. Try to improve a specific aspect of your performance, achieve high repetition, and get immediate feedback.

Self-Regulation as a Component of Deliberate Practice

Self-regulation also begins with setting goals. The best performers set goals that are not just about the outcome, but also about the process of attaining the outcome. The best performers make specific, technique-oriented plans. The best performers also go into their work with a powerful belief in their ability to produce the accomplishments. During the work, the most important self-regulatory skill that top performers use is self-observation. They are, in effect, able to step outside themselves, monitor what is happening in their own minds, and ask how it's going.

Researchers call this metacognition—knowledge about your own knowledge, or thinking about your own thinking. The practice opportunities that we find in work won't do any good if we don't evaluate them afterwards. Excellent performers judge themselves differently from the way other people perform self-evaluations. They're more specific, just as they are when they set goals and strategies.

As you add to your knowledge domain, your objective is not just to amass information. You are building a mental model, a picture of how your domain functions as a system. This is one of the defining traits of great performers: they all possess large, highly developed, intricate mental models of their domains.

Rich mental models contribute to great performance in three major ways:

- A mental model forms the framework on which you arrange your growing expertise.
- A mental model helps you distinguish relevant information from irrelevant information.
- Most important, a mental model enables you to anticipate what will happen next.

Continued deliberate practice enables exemplary performers to maintain skills that would otherwise decline with age and to develop additional skills and strategies to compensate for declines that can no longer be avoided. We've seen business people performing at the highest levels at advanced ages. Warren Buffett continues to run Berkshire Hathaway brilliantly in his 80s. As another example, when Grandma Moses contracted arthritis in her mid-70s, she found holding a brush easier than holding a needle, so she switched "professions" from creating and selling embroidery work to painting. She then painted more than 1,000 canvases, many of which became classics before she died at 101. In *Reboot! What to Do When Your Career Is Over but Your Life Isn't*, Phil Burgess cites many other examples of business leaders, entrepreneurs, professional athletes, entertainers, artists, politicians, and people in other fields who were highly successful in later life because they retained their habits of deliberate practice and engagement with others.[6]

Where Does the Passion Come From?

The central question about motivation to achieve great performance is whether it's intrinsic or extrinsic. Most of us believe the drive must be ultimately intrinsic. Much of the research supports this view. The consistent finding reported by many researchers examining many domains is that *high creative achievement and intrinsic motivation go together*. The great majority of the research in business motivation has focused on what motivates employees generally, not on what drives the top performers. The drivers are almost never extrinsic. Long after executives and entrepreneurs accumulate more money than they could ever use and more fame than anyone could hope for, they keep working and trying to get better. Yet that can't be the whole story. Intrinsic motivation may dominate the picture, but everyone, even the greatest achievers, has responded to extrinsic forces at critical moments.

World-class achievers are driven to improve, but most of them didn't start out that way. If the drive to excel develops, rather than appearing fully formed, then how does it develop? Several researchers have separately proposed "the multiplier effect." The concept is simple. A very small advantage in some field can spark a series of events that produce far larger advantages. This multiplier effect accounts not just for improvement of skills over time, but also for the motivation that drives the improvement.

The concept of the multiplier effect is embedded in the concept of deliberate practice. A beginner's skills are so modest that he or she can manage only a little bit of deliberate practice, because it's highly demanding. But that little bit of practice increases the person's skills, making it possible to do more practice, which increases the person's skill level further.

Passion develops, rather than emerges suddenly and fully formed. We've also seen hints that childhood may be especially important in how the drive gets started. What would cause someone to do the enormous work necessary to be an exemplary performer? It depends on your answers to two basic questions: What do you really want? And what do you really believe? What you want is fundamental, because deliberate practice takes a heavy investment. The second question is more profound. What do you really believe? Belief can be constraining. Everyone who has achieved exceptional performance has encountered significant challenges along the way. What you really believe about the source of great performance becomes the foundation of what you achieve.

What the evidence demonstrates is striking: great performance is not reserved for a preordained few. It is available to you and to everyone.

The evidence shows that the price of top-level achievement is extraordinarily high. It's inevitable that not many people will choose to go for it. But the evidence also shows that by understanding how a few become great, *anyone can become better*. Above all, what the evidence demonstrates is striking: great performance is not reserved for a preordained few. It is available to you and to everyone.

Summary

This chapter addresses three critical characteristics of exemplary performers—motivation, intentionality, and deliberate practice. The first two are difficult to develop "from scratch" in adults and are characteristics to look for during the selection process. That's not to say that they can't be enhanced by a well-designed, supportive work system. However, hiring for these traits can give you a significant jump start in establishing exemplary performance.

The third, deliberate practice, can be "designed in" to an organization's work processes, thereby shifting the performance curve to the right. In fact, in many of the most critical roles we depend on—commercial pilots, first responders, and so forth—deliberate practice in the form of simulation is a core aspect of ongoing professional development. Our challenge is to understand why it is so sparsely used within our own organizations. Are we intentionally accepting lower levels of performance and, if so, why?

Chapter Ten will describe how to provide all of your employees with the requisite skills and knowledge in the most cost-effective and impactful way.

Notes
1. Michael Oher, *I Beat the Odds* (New York: Gotham Books, 2010), 189.
2. John Keller, *Motivational Design for Learning and Performance* (New York: Springer Science and Business Media, 2010), 44–45.
3. Oher, *I Beat the Odds*, 195.
4. Geoff Colvin, *Talent Is Overrated: What Really Separates World-Class Performers from Everybody Else* (New York: Portfolio, 2008).

5. K. A. Ericsson, "The Influence of Experience and Deliberate Practice on the Development of Superior Expert Performance," in *The Cambridge Handbook of Expertise and Expert Performance*, eds. K. A. Ericsson, N. Charness, P. J. Feltovich, and R. R. Hoffman (Cambridge: Cambridge University Press, 2006).

6. P. Burgess, *Reboot! What to Do When Your Career Is Over but Your Life Isn't* (Victoria, BC: FriesenPress, 2011).

CHAPTER TEN

Replicating Your Stars!

Training and Performance Support

Figure 10.1. The Role of Skills and Knowledge in the EPS Model

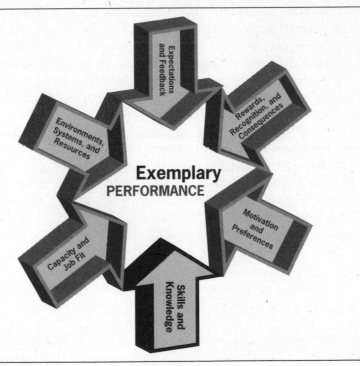

Source: Exemplary Performance, LLC. Copyright 2008–2012.

In This Chapter

- Why Training Is Not the Default Tool for Improving Incumbent Performance
- Where to Store Required Skills, Knowledge, and Procedural Information
- Designing, Developing, and Delivering Context-Intensive Training
- Developing and Implementing Performance Support

In Chapter Four we discussed how to capture the DNA of your exceptionally high performers. A significant component of their DNA is their rich mental models of how they produce exceptional results. A high percentage of these powerful mental models are the skills, knowledge, and information that your stars apply within the work process, as seen in Figure 10.1.

Well-designed training is an effective and efficient tool for transferring the requisite skills, knowledge, and information to workers who are newly assigned to a role. We consider well-designed training to have the following characteristics:

- The structure of the training should precisely mirror how your stars produce exemplary results.
- The content should align with actual work practices.
- Rich, role-specific examples and practices should be included.
- Sufficient practice is provided to support skills transfer to the work setting.
- An explicit decision must be made between storing the information in the memory of the performer or making it available through performance support.
- The training concludes with a simulation of the critical work processes at the highest level of fidelity that is practical.[1]

When new-hire training is designed and developed, based on a Profile of Exemplary Performance captured from your star performers, we consistently see impressive results. For example, ramp-up times for new hires are reduced by 30% or more.

Concurrently, training design, development, and delivery times are all shortened by 20% to 40%. The combination of faster ramp-up times and reduced training cycles has a significant impact on the value that new hires produce in the early months of their employment.

We won't dwell on this positive impact of context-intensive training for on-boarding new hires. We will merely say that, although training is absolutely essential for new hires, you shouldn't assume (and management often does) that training is the key tool for improving the performance of incumbents. Clearly, this is an inaccurate assumption.

Why Training Is Not the Default Tool for Improving Incumbent Performance

Historically, productivity has been a strong predictor of a business's success. Although this construct has typically been applied to manufacturing, it is also now used when discussing knowledge work. Manufacturing production constitutes an increasingly smaller proportion of the U.S. economy. Currently, it employs less than 10% of the workforce. On the other hand, more than 70% of the workforce is now tied to knowledge and services industries, where productivity has stagnated, despite massive investments in information technology. Clearly, moving the productivity needle forward represents a substantial opportunity.

One of the factors contributing to this suboptimal improvement in productivity is management's overreliance on training as the principal tool for improving performance. When deciding whether training is an appropriate intervention to improve performance within your workforce, you should consider three important issues.

The first issue begins with a simple question: *Is the target audience performing a required task correctly some of the time?* In our work across scores of organizations, the answer to this question is almost always yes. When the answer is yes, it is clear that the target audience has the requisite skills and knowledge. If work is being performed correctly on Tuesday and doesn't meet the standards on Wednesday, it's not due to a lack of skills and knowledge. All the training in the world will not improve the performance of an employee group with this variability in performance.

The second factor has to do with a simple statistic reality. Evidence from multiple studies across the past two decades indicate that, when incumbents are underperforming, 10% to 12% of the performance gap is attributed to skill, knowledge, and information deficiencies. The rest of the deficiency is attributed to *other factors within the work system.*

This leads to the third factor, which is an issue of *alignment of the work systems.* To optimally shift the performance curve, you must align the six performance system components shown in Figure 10.2 (and introduced initially in Chapter One). There is a basic principle within systems thinking that states that, if you optimize a subsystem, you suboptimize the overall system. What this means is that if you default to training as the sole solution for improving performance and pour all of your resources into that single solution, even if the training is perfect, optimal results will never be achieved.

Figure 10.2. Aligning the Subsystems

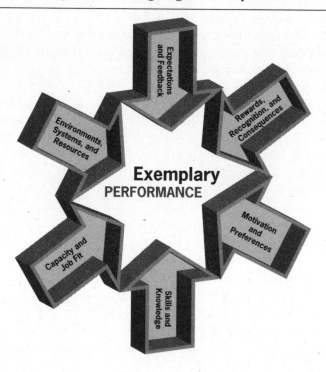

Often management relies too heavily on training as a universal response to inadequate performance. Further, managers frequently confuse training with learning, losing sight of the fact that training is in large measure an attempt to standardize work. Unfortunately, such an intervention frequently works against innovation and the creation of new knowledge, which is foundational for knowledge and service workers. In fact, you can fairly assume that knowledge and service workers learn best when they are

> *Knowledge workers learn best when they are performing actual work, facing real challenges, and producing meaningful results.*

performing actual work, facing real challenges, and producing meaningful results. Yes, classroom-based learning may be helpful, but only to the degree that it closely resembles the actual work situation, and when there is well-designed support on the job to transfer what is learned in class.

Where to Store Required Skills, Knowledge, and Procedural Information

When analysis determines that performance is deficient due to lack of skills or knowledge, you must decide which alternative for storing information is most effective for producing results. The options are to store the information in the memory of the performers or to store the information externally in what is referred to as performance support.[2]

Performance support is a class of tools that provide requisite knowledge and information, just in time at point of need. Imagine visiting your local automated teller machine (ATM) to withdraw cash. But instead of finding the usual visual cues to help you select an account and indicate an amount, you had to attend a bank-sponsored training program until you could punch in a series of numerical commands from memory. Or to further illustrate the concept, imagine this familiar scenario *with* performance support that we all rely on nearly every day: leaving a voice mail message. Just imagine trying to leave an urgent message on a voice mail system without audio prompts to direct you, requiring you to guess which numerical command was correct.

Performance support is a storage place for information, other than memory, that is used while performing a task.

Performance support is a storage place for information, other than memory, that is used *while* performing a task. It provides a signal to the performer on when to carry out increments of a task, which reduces the amount of recall necessary and minimizes error. Performance support can appear as simple instructions to assemble equipment or complex algorithms to analyze systems. This includes tools such as checklists, decision tables, performance-centric user interfaces, embedded help systems (such as the voice mail example), job aids, and so on.

The decision whether to use performance support or long-term memory is a trade-off because each has advantages and disadvantages. Advantages of long-term memory include the following:

- Long-term memory allows performers to act quickly (within seconds), and this usually translates into higher productivity.
- The performer's hands and eyes are unencumbered.
- Performers are likely to be given more credit by other people (bosses, peers, customers) if they can respond without external aid. Often these people equate competence with speed and memory, rather than just the quality of the performance.
- In rare cases, memory storage is mandated by regulations.

The disadvantages of long-term memory storage include the following:

- Despite good teaching tactics, decline in retention begins within seconds and can be serious within hours. When the interval between learning and on-the-job practice is long, loss of retention often wipes out any performance improvement, unless performance support is used.
- There is greater variability of performance for memory-based activities.
- Variables such as task interference, personal problems, and prior learning can hinder job performers from accessing long-term memory.
- The instructional design and development of training materials takes much longer to produce than performance support, resulting in higher development costs.

- Training time for long-term memory storage is greater, resulting in higher delivery costs. The delivery cost of training typically exceeds all other costs combined.
- Higher retraining costs occur when there is a change in the work process. Unlearning then relearning is one of the more expensive problems faced by trainers and educators.

If you determine that long-term memory storage is *not* the best information storage alternative, you can develop performance support. Performance support is not limited to a particular type of task. It has been developed for linear tasks such as equipment assembly and filling out forms, but has also been developed for complex tasks such as medical diagnosis, business negotiation, and the analysis of complex systems. The amount of information available in performance support is not limited; performance support can be one sentence or pages of information embedded in an information system.

The following *job tasks* are ideal candidates for performance support:

- A task performed with relatively low frequency;
- A highly complex task. A task is complex if fine discrimination of stimuli is involved, such as a fighter pilot determining whether an oncoming aircraft is friend or foe, or if there is a series of binary discriminations, such as inspecting or troubleshooting a complex electronic system;
- A task with criteria which, if not met, results in high consequence of error, such as high financial loss, injury, or loss of life (such as an engineer designing a chemical plant); and
- A task with a high probability of change in the future. That is, the way in which the task is being currently performed is likely to change because of changes in technology, policy, or equipment. In such cases, other variables being equal, it is often not worth devoting time and other resources in the costly, time-consuming process of training. It is far more cost-efficient to update a performance support tool than to retrain a portion of the workforce.

Characteristics of the task do not rule out the use of performance support. Some tasks have severe time requirements in which even seconds matter. For example, the initial actions of a pilot during an in-flight emergency must be immediate rather than guided by performance support. Note that pilots are trained to shift to performance support (flight procedures) immediately after taking the initial corrective actions. Why? These actions are infrequently performed, are highly complex, and may have devastating consequences.

Another inhibiting factor might be the performance environment. For example, a surgeon might face the problem of how to ensure that a performance support tool is kept sterile. Social barriers might be another inhibiting factor in the use of performance support. For example, if more credit is given by bosses, peers, and customers for the use of long-term memory storage (knowing all product prices or order numbers), the job performer might not use performance support, no matter how complex the task.

Figure 10.3 provides the logic for making the decision between performance support and training to memory. We have been using this tool for decades and find that it produces consistently valid results. The most interesting aspect of this tool is the conclusion that performance support is the preferred option over training.

Figure 10.3. Job Aid Versus Memory Decision

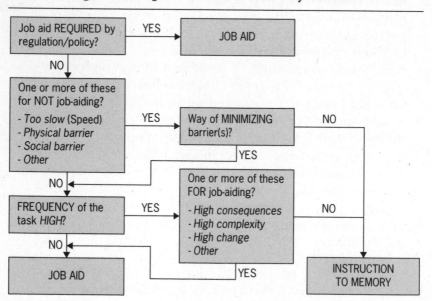

This is the reverse of all the assumptions that most managers and training organizations have in regard to the most effective and efficient way to provide skills and knowledge to performers. We believe, however, that it is always preferable to provide performance support over training, when you have reached this conclusion based on data about the actual nature of the work. If this seems counterintuitive to you, remember that the costs of developing performance support are significantly less and delivered in much less time than the equivalent training.

Designing, Developing, and Delivering Context-Intensive Training

When training (to memory) is required, we are strong advocates for context-intensive training. Context-intensive training is designed directly from the Profile of Exemplary Performance discussed in Chapter Four. The structure of the training is analogous to the work structure/process. The examples and practices are role specific and include the current best approaches captured from exemplary performers and teams. Figure 10.4 shows the structure of a sales role on the left and the corresponding curriculum model on the right.

Figure 10.4. Relationship Between Profile of Exemplary Performance and Context-Intensive Training Curriculum

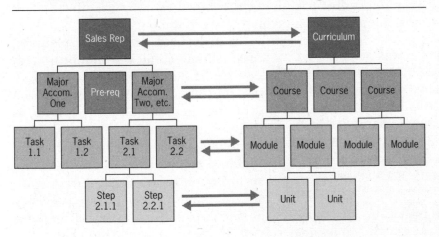

Because participants never have to ask how the training relates to their work, this context-intensive design model drives measures of relevance and training transfer off scale!

If one of the accomplishments for the role is "Accurate forecast," the corresponding course on the right would be entitled "How to Produce an Accurate Forecast." If a key task for producing accurate forecasts is "Analyze competitive landscape," you would need a module entitled "How to Analyze the Competitive Landscape." Because participants never have to ask how the training relates to their work, this context-intensive design model drives measures of relevance and training transfer off scale!

When approaching the design and development of instruction, you should remember that this arena is strewn with wasteful, ineffective practices. For example:

- Providing a group of trainees with the same information for a fixed amount of time without regard to individual needs;
- Grading on a curve; or
- Using multiple-choice questions as a tool for assessing the trainees' ability to produce accomplishments or results, versus using an appropriate level of simulation or actual on-the-job practice.

Unfortunately, these ineffective practices are such a part of the mythology of what constitutes "good" training that it is often impossible to dislodge these myths with more effective and efficient practices based on sound research.

The purpose of instructional design: to prescribe instruction that will teach the learner to perform as the role requires and, at the same time, to adjust to the needs of the individual.

Instructional design is a planning process that creates a blueprint that developers can use as a guide for drafting the instructional materials, along with the methodology to be used to deliver those materials. Many ways exist to design instruction and develop the required components to deliver it, but regardless of the mix selected, the purpose remains the same: to prescribe instruction that will teach the learner to perform as the role requires and, at the same time, to adjust to the needs of the individual.

In effect, this means you should provide instruction and practice only in those skills and tasks not yet mastered and only as much training as is needed to produce the level of competence required for the role. This context-intensive model will enhance the trainees' motivation to apply what was learned to his or her world of work. The training should also guarantee to produce graduates able to perform to the level as described in the Profile of Exemplary Performance and yet be flexible enough to avoid the enormous waste associated with a one-size-fits-all design approach.

Why do we stress the importance of designing the training based on the information captured from your exemplary performers? To do this requires a little background information as to the difference between *declarative knowledge* and *procedural knowledge*. Declarative knowledge is often described as "knowing what" and procedural knowledge is described as "knowing how."

> You can learn everything there is to know about a subject, but still not be able to use that knowledge to do anything.

If you know how to use a copier, you have procedural knowledge. If you know the underlying principles concerning how a copier works, you have declarative knowledge. There is significant evidence that declarative knowledge is different from procedural knowledge. You can learn everything there is to know about a subject, but still not be able to use that knowledge to do anything. For example, learning the rules of grammar may help you learn the Italian language, but being able to state the rules does not mean you can speak the language. Speaking requires procedural knowledge.

Experts aren't just faster and more accurate than novices or incumbents who are performing at a lower level—they know more and different aspects of the problem, and they have insights that the novice cannot yet fully understand. In fact, six major differences exist between experts and nonexperts that are important to consider in the design of instruction.

1. In general, experts have more specific declarative knowledge. They have more principles in their mental models, and those principles operate more automatically. This allows them to synthesize their declarative knowledge and apply it more systematically to the procedures that require it.

2. Experts have better links between their declarative knowledge (mental models) and their procedural structures. These links allow them to bring principles and procedures together to solve problems more efficiently.
3. Experts are really exceptional at organizing their mental models. Solving a new problem involves constructing and manipulating that mental model and, in the process, making more associations among the declarative and procedural knowledge structures. This ability provides them with mental shortcuts that make the experts highly efficient.
4. Experts categorize and group problems differently than less experienced performers do. They are able to extract the abstract problem features from the surface symptoms they encounter and categorize those features based on their deep mental models.
5. Experts frequently generate heuristics (strategies) for solving problems by working forward from the initial condition or problem, generating a hypothesis for a solution, and then applying the new solution to see if it leads to the desired goal.
6. And finally, experts are more likely to persist if the first strategy doesn't work. A novice may give up after an initial failure.

Based on this research, the challenge for training is to assist learners to categorize problems the way experts do and to build an appropriate mental model of the work that contains all the correct components, in the right relationships, with the right operating principles. This is the logic behind a context-intensive approach to training design.

Using Structured On-the-Job Training

Structured on-the-job training (SOJT) is an approach to training design and implementation that produces a rich, context-intensive approach. This is an approach we often recommend. But first, it is important to differentiate between SOJT and unstructured on-the-job training.

In North America, on-the-job training (OJT) is most commonly used to refer to a haphazard and ineffective approach of pairing a novice with a more experienced performer. The hope is that, through osmosis, the right information will pass at the right time from the more experienced performer to the less experienced performer. It is typically not systematic, replicable, scalable, or dependable. Unstructured OJT leads to trainees acquiring skills through the following means:

- Impromptu explanations and demonstrations by others, whether or not those providing the information are qualified performers. The research shows that when subject-matter experts serve as ad hoc coaches, they leave out 70% of the process steps that the novice requires to be successful;
- Self-initiated trial-and-error efforts; and
- Random imitation of others' behavior, regardless of whether they are qualified to serve as examples.

In contrast, SOJT is defined as the planned process of developing task-level expertise by pairing an experienced employee with a less experienced employee, at or near the actual work setting. The discrete job tasks that are documented and observed serve as the basis for the training content and objectives.

SOJT is only as effective as the experienced and knowledgeable employees who serve as the trainers. These SOJT trainers should demonstrate adequate competence in the work being presented and in the skills required to present that work to others. Therefore, in SOJT the development of trainers is often a formal, extensive process in and of itself.

Regardless of the delivery method, context-intensive training provides multiple benefits. Training is highly relevant, lean, and transfers to the work setting effectively and efficiently.

Developing and Implementing Performance Support

Would you feel safe getting on an airplane knowing that the crew had gone through their preflight routine entirely from memory? What if the company installing a sprinkler system in your new office skipped the post-installation checklist because their workers have done the installation hundreds of times before?

In the workplace, it would be unthinkable for employees to "wing it" in many situations, no matter their experience level.

Training to memory usually takes about three times as long and costs two to three times as much as the equivalent performance support covering the same material.

Performance support enables employees to perform tasks more accurately and reliably and to acquire new skills more quickly. In addition, performance support is quicker and less costly than formal training that has memory storage as its objective. Training to memory usually takes about three times as long and costs two to three times as much as the equivalent performance support covering the same material. If the task in question has a high probability of a change in methodology, it is easier to revise a performance support than develop a new training course.

Any performance support must directly guide the task, address only those skills relevant to job performance, and be cost-effective. The following outlines how to develop and implement performance support as part of your performance improvement solution.

Task 1: Collect data about the work. You need information concerning any regulations requiring performance support, the speed of performance, physical conditions, social conditions, frequency, the consequence of error, complexity, and the probability of change for the task.

Task 2: Select storage alternatives. Choose among performance support only, long-term memory storage only, performance support plus supporting instruction, or instruction plus prompting performance support.

Task 3: Determine whether barriers to performance support can be overcome. When a barrier to a performance support is present, sometimes it can be minimized or outweighed by the potential benefits. For example, in the case of the speed of performance barrier, a special job aid might be developed that serves as a prompt for recalling information that has been previously stored in memory. These serve as "memory joggers" and can take the form of outlines, key words, flow charts, or schematic drawings. These prompting tools are placed in the work environment in such a manner that consulting them will not slow the speed of response. Examples include wall charts, laminated pocket cards, and labels on machinery.

Task 4: Determine whether training support is needed. It is rare for performance support to stand on its own without being introduced in some formal way. Simply preparing performance support and sending it out to the intended audience has not met with as much success as introducing the support in briefings or, more typically, by building training seminars and courses on how to use the aid.

   If the situation permits, self-instructional materials can be developed so that a formal training session is not necessary. These materials should provide the reader with practice exercises in using the performance support.

Task 5: Develop performance support. The performance support should be built according to specifications and guided by known rules for impacting behavior and theories on how humans process information.

Task 6: Test performance support. You need to determine whether the job performer produces the desired accomplishment as a result of using the performance support. Tryouts (developmental tests) should be carried out one-on-one with employees for whom the performance support is designed. Then conduct a formal validation test of the performance support. Finally, conduct a follow-up evaluation that answers these questions:

- Did the performance support solve or minimize the problem by satisfying the need specified in the analysis?
- Did the value produced by the performance support exceed the cost of development and implementation?[3]

Performance support can be delivered via various technologies. For example, laminated seat pocket cards detailing emergency procedures and equipment are used in airplanes. "Wizards" and cue cards are embedded in complex software. Audio cues are used to prompt the steps in leaving a voice mail message. In each case, the designer has selected an appropriate technology to support performance.

A task characteristic with a high consequence of error might drive you toward electronic performance support. For example, someone might use an electronic worksheet when mixing hazardous materials in a plant. The advantage over a paper worksheet is the ability to eliminate calculation errors while providing written or audio warnings at key points in the process.

Along with the characteristics of the task, the availability of the technology should be considered. If the target audience has ready access to information technology or is already using a computer while performing the task, electronic performance support can be a cost-effective intervention.

Harless (2001) reported the following outcomes based on case studies involving job aids and performance support:

- A one-week training course for an electronics manufacturer was reduced to one day with an accompanying eight-page performance support. Performance proficiency increased by 50%.
- A chemical company reduced errors in insecticide formulation from 10% to 1% by using a two-page performance support.
- A company found no significant difference in performance between an experienced group of technicians designated as experts and an inexperienced group of technicians who employed a performance support in troubleshooting a system.[4]

Summary

Well-designed training is an effective and efficient tool for transferring the requisite skills, knowledge, and information to people newly assigned to a role. The problem is that management holds an unfounded assumption that training is the key tool for improving the performance of incumbents. When analysis determines that performance is deficient due to lack of skills or knowledge, you must decide which alternative for storing information is most effective for producing results. The options are to store the information in the memory of the performers or to store the information externally, in what we refer to as performance support.

When training to memory is required, we are strong advocates for context-intensive training. Context-intensive training is designed directly from the Profile of Exemplary Performance discussed in Chapter Four. The structure of the training is analogous to the work structure or process. The purpose of designing the instruction is to prescribe instruction that will teach the learner to perform as the role requires and, at the same time, to adjust to the needs of the individual.

Structured on-the-job training (SOJT) is a highly recommended approach to training design and implementation that produces a rich, context-intensive approach and is defined by its use of experienced and knowledgeable employees with the right skills who serve as the trainers. Regardless of the delivery method, context-intensive training is a relevant, efficient, lean, and effective approach to shifting your stars' expertise to the solid performers, thereby shifting the performance curve.

Finally, performance support yields more accurate and reliable job performance, is less expensive to develop than instruction, and dramatically reduces formal training time. It should be considered in every project in which prior analysis shows a need for information.

Notes
1. J. H. Harless, *Accomplishment-Based Curriculum Development System* (Redwood Shores, CA: Saba, 2001).
2. P. H. Elliott, "Job Aids," in *Handbook of Human Performance Technology*, eds. H. D. Stolovitch and E. J. Keeps (San Francisco: Pfeiffer, 1999).
3. J. H. Harless, *Job Aids Workshop* (Redwood Shores, CA: Saba, 2001).
4. Ibid.

CHAPTER ELEVEN

Getting Round Pegs in Round Holes

Selecting for Success

Figure 11.1. The Role of Capacity and Job Fit in the EPS Model

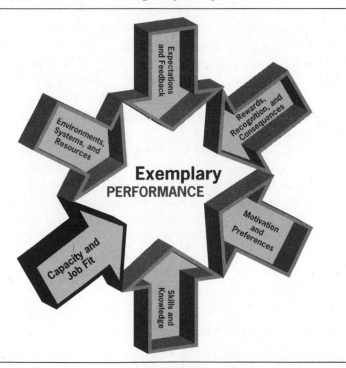

Source: Exemplary Performance, LLC. Copyright 2008–2012.

In this chapter, we'll discuss the importance of capacity and job fit to exemplary performance (Figure 11.1).

Do you know any talented people who are average performers? Of course you do! Do you know of any teams with lots of talent that don't perform? The imagery of forcing a square peg into a round hole is an easily adapted metaphor to hiring processes. Everyone wants a new hire to be a good fit. In reality, many square pegs are hired, and those new employees (and the organizations that hired them) struggle with this poor fit. We also realize that jobs and people are not simply geometric shapes and that an individual's success in an organization involves a complex set of variables. Hiring and selection processes are typically part of what are called human resources processes, talent management, or human capital management. In McKinsey's *The War for Talent*,[1] the argument is made that people (the "talent") are of strategic importance to the success of the organization. We certainly agree. The challenge we have seen is in how organizations go about this strategically important process.

Most selection processes are based on capability or potential to perform. There is an underlying assumption that talented, high-potential hires will end up being exemplary performers. Unfortunately, this simply is not a valid assumption. One way to think about the hiring process is by associating information about the job or position as the "requirements" and those persons who would be successful hires as the "solutions." With that premise in mind, this chapter begins with a discussion about how some organizations define job requirements.

Defining Job Requirements

If every variable about a particular job were identified as part of the requirements, you would then have one unique description for every position in the organization. Although this may even be reasonable in some micro-sized businesses, it is not practical in most. Sometimes the position description is formulated around the person who just vacated the job. Acknowledging that certain aspects cannot be included in the job description, there's a tendency to generalize. The HR department has either created a list of competencies or has adopted a competency framework, and line managers can then associate parts of that framework to the vacant position and build a competency-based selection model.

> The problem with typical job requirements is that each step in the logic chain is an approximation or estimate.

Typically, job requirements are built through simple job analysis or an online survey answered by representative samples of job experts, incumbents, or managers. Once gathered, this information is used to build a formal talent assessment program. The problem with this approach is that each step in the logic chain is an approximation or estimate. The further we stray from well-defined performance (producing accomplishments that have value to the organization), the less likely we are to find a great job fit. Talent and potential are, at best, correlated with high performance, but not causative.

> Talent and potential are, at best, correlated with high performance, but not causative.

In a recent article, Pepitone and Wyatt noted that many talent management systems and tools used to select, support, and retain employees were conceived 60 years ago and no longer serve their intended purpose.[2] Even more recent tools that directly support recruiting use either outdated knowledge to provide the support or have been "gamed" to a degree that makes them ineffective or hopeless. The authors point out that the continuing use of these methods, though convenient, reduces the effectiveness of management and recruiting.

SAT Example

The familiar Scholastic Achievement Test (SAT) required by most colleges and universities for admission is a good example of our reliance on using standardized testing to predict performance. Research has repeatedly shown that the SAT score accounts for only 10% to 20% of the variance in college student success.[3] We are not arguing for or against these tests, but are rather using the SAT scores to make a point. What do universities want from their students? Good citizenship, scholarly effort, and ability to learn at a pace within the institutions' norms. Clearly, the SAT may be a good measure of some aspects of learning, but in reality not with the precision that many assume. In addition, good citizenship means being engaged in curricular and extracurricular activities and conducting personal behavior within societal norms. Scholarly effort means doing assignments and participating in class and study groups. That's why many universities have adopted the "whole person" view in making admission decisions.

How, then, could we expect a paper-and-pencil (or online) battery of questions to reliably predict a set of interpersonal skills or other job competencies that might in turn predict success on the job? More direct measures of potential to perform should be used. That's why we propose an alternative method that includes the following elements:

- Identifying the on-the-job accomplishments that people should produce;
- Seeking new hires who have successfully produced those accomplishments under similar conditions; and
- Evaluating potential new hires against the criteria associated with existing exemplary performers occupying the position to be filled.

Job fit is also about "truth in advertising."

How does this theoretical new hire "best-case" scenario play out in both private and government sectors? How do organizations use job fit—or selection and assignment—as critical factors in job performance? How do you turn the outputs of performance analysis into hiring and assignment actions? The next part of this chapter discusses this topic and provides related examples.

Providing Clarity

Job fit is about the selection and assignment of people, but it is also about "truth in advertising." Organizations have policies and procedures about hiring and filling positions. There are human resources structures such as job descriptions and, in large organizations, there are occupational series, job classifications, labor categories, and even bargaining unit agreements that specify some of these same artifacts. Why do organizations use these? Because it helps organize, categorize, and shape the organizational chart, providing easier means for doing the "accounting" of human resources. The generalizations that occur allow those without the functional expertise to manage the hiring or selection process.

The result of adhering to these processes can be that the job description used in a hiring decision is a far reach from the actual job requirements. This spells trouble from the start, as the initial search for candidates does not exactly match what the organization requires. There is also the less obvious implication that those seeking the position are not clear about their own fit.

For example, one organization sought to identify a qualified candidate for a managing director whose job description read like a facility manager: "responsible for oversight of operations, costs, and production." In truth, the role of managing director included a significant sales component. For those who interviewed for the job, there were frustration and confusion when asked about their sales experience. You can also imagine there were others who would have been a great fit, with sales experience and success, who did not show any interest because the job advertisement said nothing about sales responsibility.

In one of our projects, we examined the role of commercial insurance underwriters. To determine the value produced by underwriters, we developed a list of job accomplishments produced by exemplary performers. Table 11.1 is a side-by-side comparison of the *job description* of commercial insurance underwriters versus *the outputs produced* by the best commercial insurance underwriters in this organization.

In addition to the accomplishments shown on the right side of the table, we also collected detailed information about the criteria used to assess each of those outputs, as well as the actions or activities involved in producing each of these outputs. For

Table 11.1. Commercial Insurance Underwriter Job Description Versus Major Accomplishments

Job Description	Major Accomplishments
• Authorize reinsurance of policy when risk is high • Decline excessive risks • Decrease value of policy when risk is substandard • Evaluate possibility of losses due to catastrophe or excessive insurance • Examine documents to determine degree of risk from such factors as applicant financial standing and value and condition of property	• Actionable business plan • Network of brokers and clients to support business plan • Competitive proposals • Profitable book of business

hiring purposes, managers can stay at this level of detail and ask candidates:

- For examples of actionable business plans produced in their past role(s);
- To describe their professional networks and past interactions with clients and brokers; and
- To explain their "book of business" in previous positions and how they influenced that book of business in positive directions.

You might also conclude from the job description on the left that commercial insurance underwriters carry out their responsibilities without interacting with clients or brokers. However, we observed that these exemplary performers scheduled upwards of 100 personal contacts each year with brokers.

Military Example

In the military, determining job fit is a unique challenge. Even prior to showing up at boot camp, new recruits undergo a battery of tests known as the Armed Services Vocational Aptitude Battery (ASVAB). These tests include such assessments as arithmetic reasoning, mathematical skills, reading comprehension, and mechanical skills. Career field selection then becomes a function of individual choice among the career fields in which the recruit is qualified and the openings in those career fields within the respective branch of the Armed Forces. Specific assignments following initial occupational training are a result of the person's interest and an umbrella concept called "needs of the service," involving many factors, which range from past performance to geographic preference to colocation with a military spouse.

At any particular unit, however, more specific job assignment decisions are made. If you recall our previous U.S. Coast Guard weapons petty officer (WPO) example in Chapter Three, you'll note that the assignment as WPO at hundreds of smaller units is not directly connected to the person's specific occupational specialty. Table 11.2 provides a side-by-side comparison of gunner's mates (occupational specialty that fills these roles at larger units) training versus the accomplishments that weapons petty officers should produce.

As an example, one of the major accomplishments of the weapons petty officer is to produce sufficient weapons-qualified

Table 11.2. Weapons Petty Officer Job Description Versus Major Accomplishments

Job Description	Major Accomplishments
<ul><li>Clean weapons</li><li>Conduct PMS</li><li>Inventory weapons and ammo</li><li>Keep records</li><li>Maintain security</li></ul>	<ul><li>Sufficient weapons-qualified unit personnel</li><li>Service-ready weapons, ammunition, and pyrotechnics</li><li>Required administrative documentation</li><li>Satisfactory annual ordnance inspections</li><li>Proper materiel condition of ordnance and armory spaces</li><li>Proper response to missing, lost, or stolen weapons, ammo, or pyro</li><li>Proper response to weapons-related mishaps</li></ul>

unit personnel. Knowing how to teach someone to shoot a weapon is not sufficient. Training people to shoot accurately is not sufficient. Producing the results where there are a sufficient number of qualified persons at the unit to carry out the law enforcement mission today is an output that provides value not only to the unit but to the organization.

Leveraging Job Accomplishments in Selection

Having established where value accrued to the organization by the outputs of weapons petty officers, we can now align selection criteria for assigning people to this role. As we discussed, those who are not in the occupational specialty of gunner's mate fill collateral duty WPO positions. Traditionally, this "part-time" job is filled with 2nd class petty officers (E-5 pay grade) in the boatswain's mate occupational specialty. What this means is that for the population from which we are drawing WPOs, we have experienced operators who have been out on boats conducting law enforcement and search-and-rescue operations. They bring with them the reality check of what is required to get the job done. As we narrow this population down to those who would perform best as WPOs, we look for those who have a particular affinity with guns, have fired weapons accurately, cleaned and maintained weapons themselves (quite likely their own), and handled ammunition as a matter of routine. Additional selection criteria come from examining each of the other major accomplishments.

Having established where value accrued to the organization by the outputs, we can now align selection criteria.

Pathologist Example

Even highly specialized jobs such as a clinical pathologist are well served by first identifying major accomplishments and then selecting individuals based on their experience of producing those accomplishments to standards or criteria identified from exemplary performers.

If you were interested in becoming a pathologist and researched what it is that pathologists do or looked for employment notices seeking clinical pathologists, you would likely find something similar to what we have listed in the left column of Table 11.3. However, our performance analysis of the role of clinical pathologists at a large commercial employer of pathologists revealed the list of major accomplishments shown in the right column of Table 11.3. These outputs were drawn from spending time observing the practices and interviewing the most highly regarded and value-producing pathologists in the company.

If we follow one of the major accomplishments listed, you'll see the paradox. In the organization we were following, the clinical pathologists were responsible for the labs that test blood, urine, and other samples. The clients from whom these samples come were either physicians or hospitals and not the individual patients. It is the pathologist who can speak to a fellow professional (medical doctor) credibly and discuss lab procedures, capabilities, and quality assurance. When a client is "on the fence" about whether to use this lab or some other facility, who better than the pathologist to inform and win him or her over? In addition, when the lab provides results that don't make sense to the client physician, it is the pathologist who can provide a collegial consult, explain the meaning of the results, and recommend follow-up tests or procedures. If a test result is "inconclusive," the pathologist can

Table 11.3. Clinical Pathologist Job Description Versus Major Accomplishments

Job Description	Major Accomplishments
• Studies nature, cause, and development of diseases and structural and functional changes caused by them • Makes diagnoses from body tissue, fluids, secretions, and other specimens • Determines presence and stage of disease, utilizing laboratory procedures • May perform autopsies to determine nature and cause of disease or death	• Increased revenue, due to winning over clients and physicians from results and personal visits • Quality assurance program for laboratory • High-performing team • Credible adviser to physicians (clients)

explain to the physician why it is so and make recommendations about whether to retest or resample. Following this description of pathologist activities, areas clearly emerge in which the pathologist's performance influences revenue, whether it is to win over new clients or retain existing relationships.

Consider the people who become clinical pathologists: very bright and capable individuals who have successfully made it through medical school and ensuing residencies of specialized training. At some point, they chose to specialize in a medical field where they do not typically interact with patients. Most would not be a good fit for having a sales component in their responsibilities. And by personality, this is likely a difficult trait for most pathologists to acquire. Herein lies one of the critical aspects of getting job fit or selection "right." Sometimes it is not something you can easily fix if you get it wrong.

> A critical aspect of getting job fit "right" is that it is not easily fixed if you get it wrong.

We encountered many pathologists who knew of their revenue-generation responsibilities and still stated, "I hate meeting with clients." Others flatly stated that they had nothing to do with revenue at their facility. In summary, what we saw here was great variance in the performance of pathologists when it came to producing some of the outputs of value for the organization. We also saw that the most cost-effective lever in improving performance was to get things right during the hiring process—to make it explicitly known that the role of pathologist in this organization carries with it revenue-generating responsibilities. Certainly doing so limits the field of candidates, but the upside is that potential candidates are narrowed to a group that will be a better fit for the organization.

Military Reserves Example

The reserve components of the U.S. Armed Forces play a vital role in serving the national defense of the United States. At times these volunteers have had the moniker of "weekend warriors," but in recent years, operations in Iraq and Afghanistan and other places throughout the world have required unprecedented mobilizations and deployments of reserve members. However, when not mobilized, their work schedules are part-time, typically serving one weekend each month and two weeks each summer on active duty for training.

One of the challenges in this nonmobilized state is to get people *ready* to deploy and to *maintain* that readiness when interactions between reservist and the organization are only once each month. Recently, a new role was established to directly support this effort, called the senior enlisted reserve adviser (SERA). Those in the SERA role are themselves reserve members who likewise have full-time employment, typically in the private sector. The official description for the role of SERAs included action verbs or phrases such as coordinate . . . stay informed about . . . monitor . . . advise command . . . provide guidance.

We are picking on the verbs because it seems rather difficult to hold someone accountable for not doing any of the above. We instead asked questions such as: What is it that this person will produce and How will you select individuals to fill this role? As in other examples, we started by focusing on the organizational goal and then sought out the outputs of value that someone in this role would produce. After meeting with key stakeholders, we were able to identify that the overall job accomplishment that someone in a SERA role should produce: *mobilization-ready reserve members at their unit.*

We then examined readiness data to answer the following questions:

- Which units were best achieving this result already?
- Who were the persons responsible for doing so?
- How were they accomplishing this result?

We found exemplary performers (albeit with different titles) who produced this result consistently. We then broke this job accomplishment into the major outputs of value to produce Figure 11.2.

By definition in the title of this job, persons selected for this position are senior in both rank and experience. One of the downsides of the official job description was that people had the sense that the role would be simply advisory. What the organization needed were those who could produce the results

Figure 11.2. Major Outputs for Person in SERA Role

shown in Figure 11.2. True enough, some of the verbs listed in the policy statement would be accurate descriptions of some of the activities required—but providing clarity around the *accomplishment*—the output of those activities—was vital to advertising and subsequently selecting the right people for this new role.

One of the immediate implications was a realization that accomplishing these outputs would require considerable time beyond one weekend per month. Those who were unable or unwilling to produce these accomplishments would be less likely to apply for the role. Selecting new SERAs who had previously produced some or all of these accomplishments in other roles greatly increased the organization's likelihood of achieving the value proposition of the new role.

Entry-Level Decisions Example

Putting the right person in the right job, right at the start, reduced first-year turnover from 66% to 30%.

The primary rule in getting job fit right is to select persons who have previously produced the job output (that is, accomplishment) to standard. This first requires identifying what those valued accomplishments are. However, there are roles that are entry-level, where experience producing the required accomplishments is unrealistic.

Swarovski is a global producer of cut crystal and gemstones. The company operates hundreds of retail stores throughout the United States and Canada. In 2009 the company terminated 66% of new sales consultants within the first year. By "putting the right person in the right job, right at the start," this turnover was slashed in 2010 to 30% and translated into $22 million in additional sales.[4] A comparison of old and new talent management strategies tells the tale of how this was accomplished (see Table 11.4).

Some of the differences are readily apparent. For example, the new process didn't accept résumés or conduct interviews until after the new assessment test was administered. Further, this Web-enabled assessment was developed after analyzing the job role on

Table 11.4. Comparison of Old and New Hiring Processes at Swarovski

Previous Hiring Process	New Hiring Process
All of the following take place decentralized and in the following order:	*All of the following occur in the following order (assessment is centralized; hiring managers are decentralized):*
1. Recruiting	1. Assessment test administered
2. Interviewing	2. Recruiting (résumé exchanged)
3. Assessment of behavioral competencies (but did not align with competencies and skills required for sales consultant success)	3. Interviewing

the floor with sales consultants and store managers and included six simulations that mirrored the Swarovski in-store environment and emulated typical customer interactions.

For entry-level hiring, when there is little confidence in finding persons already experienced at producing the required job outputs, using these high-fidelity simulations of the requirements needed to produce the valued accomplishments can be an extremely successful strategy. In this case, the technology feature of the assessment was a definite plus, providing structure, consistency, and convenience. However, the more important aspect was building the simulation in a case-based, context-rich environment drawn from the real-world culture of this organization.

Preventing a "bad fit" hiring decision by making the accomplishments clear at the onset of the process makes a great deal of sense. The effects of not putting the right person in the right job can manifest itself in numerous ways. Without this step, pathologists may be labeled as not motivated to meet sales responsibilities or senior enlisted reserve advisers may fail because they appear unwilling to put in the time needed to accomplish the job. Fixing the problems after people are hired may be challenging at best or even result in terminations. Preventing the bad fit by making the accomplishments clear at the onset of the hiring process makes more sense.

Summary

This chapter discussed job fit and selecting people who can produce outputs of value that drive organizational results. Our next chapter is about the organization and work environment that people plug into. Is the work environment, from ergonomics to job design and work processes, structured to enable people to produce results like exemplary performers?

Notes

1. E. Michaels, H. Handfield-Jones, and B. Axelrod, *The War for Talent* (Boston: Harvard Business School Publishing, 2001).
2. James Pepitone and Robert Wyatt, "New Methods Are Needed to Improve Corporate Recruiting Effectiveness," *Journal of Corporate Recruiting Leadership*, 6, no. 7 (2011): 17–28.

3. W. J. Camara and G. Echternacht, "The SAT I and High School Grades: Utility in Predicting Success in College," *College Board Research Notes RN-10* (New York: College Entrance Examination Board, July 2000).   http://professionals.collegeboard.com/profdownload/pdf/rn10_10755.pdf
4. Ken Lahti, "Swarovski Places Employees in the Right Positions, the First Time," *Talent Management Magazine,* 7, no. 11 (November 2011): 39.

CHAPTER TWELVE

Creating Barrier-Free Work Systems

Figure 12.1. The Role of Capacity and Job Fit in the EPS Model

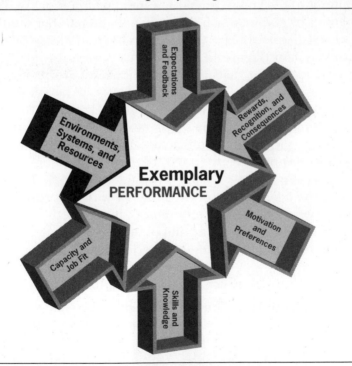

Source: Exemplary Performance, LLC. Copyright 2008–2012.

> **In This Chapter**
>
> ---
>
> • Three Major Sources of Unintended Barriers
>   • Work Design
>   • Physical Conditions
>   • Motivational Conditions

In this chapter we'll review the results of environments, systems, and resources on exemplary performance (see Figure 12.1).

In the United States the phrase "barrier-free" immediately calls to mind the Americans with Disabilities Act (ADA) of 1990, a wide-ranging civil rights law that prohibits discrimination based on disability. It includes guidance on making reasonable accommodations to the known physical or mental limitations of disabled employees by eliminating barriers that would hamper their ability to succeed at work. In fact, the ADA has been so successful that the wheelchair icon (Figure 12.2) is nearly a universal symbol around the world, indicating that unnecessary barriers have been removed.

We have found in our work with many Fortune 100 companies that most organizations don't put sufficient effort into eliminating unintended barriers to employee performance (disabled or not).

Unfortunately, we have found in our work with many Fortune 100 companies that most organizations don't put sufficient effort into eliminating unintended barriers to employee performance (disabled or not). These barriers include convoluted processes, poor ergonomics, misaligned rewards and incentives, and dozens of other unintended performance roadblocks that, when rolled up together, create a bottom-line burden no organization can afford to shoulder.

Figure 12.2. Symbol for Barrier-Free Access

Poor or inadequate "work systems" are one major drag on employee performance covered in this chapter. These work systems include organizational design, job design, process design, and myriad organizational process and control systems designed to ensure that strategic goals are realized. A well-designed system facilitates optimal performance; a poorly designed work system presents a significant barrier to achieving high performance. Our experience is that new hires are often the employees most greatly affected by these suboptimal systems.

An underlying premise of our work is our goal of enabling organizations to allow teams and individuals to be as successful as intended to be on the day they were hired or their team was formed. The newly hired are easy to spot—they are the optimistic and enthusiastic ones spreading infectious energy and commitment everywhere they go, the engaged and "glad to be here" people every organization is happy to have.

Unfortunately, all too soon that new hire's enthusiasm has dissipated—mostly due to the unintended performance barriers and inadequate work systems that organizations allow to evolve and continue. Within six months, the new hire optimism is over and, after a pitched battle, organizational reality is the hands-down victor. The vanquished new hire is forced to skulk off the workforce battlefield muttering bitterly, "How did I get myself into this mess?"

"Hold on!" you might be thinking. "My company has great processes and systems and our workforce is committed and our performance excellent." You may be correct that some systems are excellent, but we'd be willing to bet that a closer look would reveal some significant holes in the entire spectrum of work systems that have a direct impact on individual performers and teams. Our research and experience tell us that you need to align six distinct work systems to enable exemplary performance (see Figure 12.3).

These systems are

- Expectations and Feedback
- Rewards, Recognition, and Consequences
- Motivation and Preferences
- Skills and Knowledge
- Capacity and Job Fit
- Environments, Systems, and Resources

Figure 12.3. Aligning Work Systems to Support Exemplary Performance

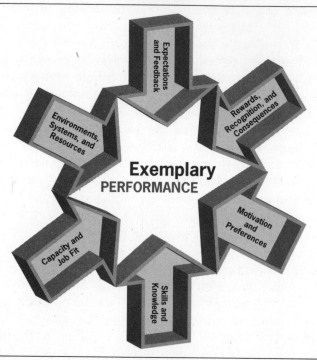

Source: Exemplary Performance, LLC. Copyright 2008–2012.

Without these support systems in place, the new-hire scenario just discussed will continue to be played out again and again. A leader's primary accountability is to be an architect who integrates and aligns work systems in order to enable high performance. To state this in another way, your primary accomplishment is to produce a powerful team of high-performing direct reports operating in a barrier-free work environment.

As the leader responsible for optimizing the performance of your team, you first need to find answers to some basic, but vitally important, questions:

- Are the performance outputs and expectations for my team aligned with those of other teams in my department or division?
- Do individual workers clearly understand how the work they perform and the results they produce contribute to shareholder value?

- Are the correct resources always available just in time?
- Do I or my team members participate in activities or meetings that do not add value or support the achievement of our objectives?

Surprisingly, our decades of combined experience tells us that most organizations have not taken the time to intentionally design the requisite systems to enable exemplary performance. Instead, what most organizations create are systems and processes that create unintended barriers and inhibit high performance.

One of our goals is to help organizations tear down these unintended barriers and enable individual performers to achieve greater business results for their organization. That is what shifting the performance curve is about.

Three Major Sources of Unintended Barriers

Unintended barriers fall into the following three categories:

- Work design, including organizational design, process design, and job design;
- Physical conditions, which includes everything from ergonomic considerations to safety; and
- Design of the motivational conditions, which include compensation, benefits, recognition, and rewards, in addition to the pace of the work, the degree of autonomy, and access to guidance and supervision.

Work Design

As noted, work design includes organizational design, job design, and process design, so let's take a closer look at each of these.

Organizational Design

The organization is the sum total of both informal and formal arrangements that support the interaction of the people, processes, and systems of the enterprise. Organizational design is intended to enhance the interface between humans and the work that the enterprise wants to accomplish. It is created both formally and informally. The intentional or unintentional design of the organization can enhance or hinder the accomplishment of the purposes of the organization. Organizational design ties together the following components:

> One of the significant errors that leaders and managers make is to attribute too many organizational problems to the failings of individual employees and far too few to the failings of the organizational design that supports them.

- *Strategic vision*: the mental picture of what the organization needs to do to compete effectively in business.
- *Structure*: how tasks are divided and coordinated, the decentralization and centralization of the enterprise, and relationships between groups and individuals.
- *Processes*: defining and measuring the steps, activities, and methods that produce a specified result, accomplishment, or output.

- *Systems*: the procedures that make the organization run using a particular set of procedures and rules, policies, devices, and so on. These are designed to control processes in a predictable way.
- *Culture*: the patterns of shared assumptions, beliefs, attitudes, expectations, and values revealed in everyday work practices. These can include formal components such as policies, processes, and procedures that influence those patterns.
- *Competence*: the way managers manage, including the way employees are selected, placed, developed, and rewarded.

To optimize performance, leaders need to align their enterprise across all these variables. This *intentional approach to organizational design* significantly reduces barriers to performance. It also harnesses all aspects of the enterprise to allow an organization to compete successfully in the global marketplace.

One of the significant errors that leaders and managers make is to attribute too many organizational problems to the failings of individual employees and far too few to the failings of the organizational design that supports them. This results in management's decision to "fix" individuals in the workplace, rather than choosing to repair and enhance the organizational structure.

When we work with clients to enhance their organizational design, we always recommend a set of solutions that include the following:

- First, understand the complexity by focusing on the whole system.
- Identify links between different structures, processes, and systems, using both quantitative and qualitative methods.
- Establish direct, comparative, and economic measures.
- Identify and eliminate work within the enterprise that does not add value directly to the desired results.

Our intent in this type of organizational design project is to align the individual employees with a work support system, so that the entire organization works more efficiently and effectively. This may include redesigning the strategic goals, objectives, and directions in order to improve long-term outcomes based on market trends and information collected from customers, leaders, and individual contributors. Process interventions are intended to improve the key processes and subprocesses and to improve the workflow of the organization as a whole.

Our intent is *not* to create the perfect organizational design, but rather to create a *self-adaptive design* that aligns the following three levels within the enterprise:

- The relationship between the external environment and the strategic direction of the enterprise;
- Work processes and technology, so that your organization's products and services are produced efficiently and in a sustainable way; and
- People, organizational structures, and HR systems that are focused on how people are organized, how authority and responsibility are distributed among them, and how employees are selected, developed, and rewarded.

By building these effective, efficient, and flexible self-adapting systems, the work processes within them become self-regulating and more responsive to the business environment. The design should also enhance employee commitment and engagement.

To be successful in this approach to organizational redesign, it's essential that the change process demonstrate and reinforce the hoped-for outcomes. *The process is more about getting the system to be adaptive than about perfecting workflow and structure.* The approach should be participative; that is, it should be undertaken by the people who must make it work.

Management can engage in this type of organizational redesign with little involvement from the employees who will be affected. The advantage of this approach is that it offers speed and produces the design that management wants. Of course, the disadvantage of this approach is that it lacks input from knowledgeable sources and may also lack support from those who will be affected by the change. The advantage of establishing a design team to lead the redesign effort is that it brings together people who are skilled in organizational design, thus allowing for the consideration of a broader set of options. Including vendors in the future design broadens options even further. However, the disadvantages of including a wide variety of stakeholders directly affected by the change means a slower design process and a smaller pool of employees involved in the effort.

However, you may decide to use a redesign effort that calls for widescale participation in the redesign by *all* key stakeholder groups. You may believe that the extended time lines and additional costs will be offset by greater buy-in and reduced resistance to the proposed change. A disadvantage is that this approach requires a large group of employees to participate in the redesign work, which makes them unavailable for their routine jobs.

Regardless of the approach taken, your work to align strategic direction, work processes, and organizational structure provides the following benefits:

- *Better coordination and information flow.* When work is organized around products and services, people who need to cooperate with each other are on the same team and are focused on a common goal.
- *Reduced costs and cycle time.* When workflow is streamlined, steps that do not add value are removed or minimized. This reduces costs, cycle time, and the opportunity for errors. When mature work teams plan and monitor their own work, fewer managers are required. The managers who remain can focus on integrating efforts across teams.

- *Improved responsiveness to customers.* When work is organized around products, services, or customer groups, employees have greater access to customers and become better at anticipating customers' needs.
- *More innovation.* When employees are given the opportunity and responsibility to improve their products, services, and processes, their ability to implement new ideas and change is significantly enhanced.
- *More flexibility.* Organizational design that is tied clearly to the vision and strategy of the company allows for change to be cascaded to the organization more smoothly and with less resistance.

Process Design

A business process is a series of steps designed to produce a product or service. Most processes are cross-functional and include handoffs between various functions of the organization. *Primary processes* result in a product or service for an external client or customer. *Support processes* may be invisible to the external client, but are essential to successfully executing the primary processes. A third category is the *management processes* that enable the primary and support processes. Each process category can be viewed as a "value chain," where each step in the process should add value to the preceding steps.

Following are some representative processes found in many companies:

- Business generation
- Product and service design
- Manufacturing
- Distribution
- Order fulfillment
- Customer service
- Budgeting
- Talent management
- Facilities management
- Purchasing
- Information management

This is, of course, a partial list, and clearly, within each of these processes are multiple subprocesses. Still, it is easy to see that if the process design of each is not optimized, then a high probability exists that your organization will underperform.

Effective processes are absolutely essential to achieving higher levels of performance and shifting the performance curve. As good as exemplary performers are at their jobs, and despite the productivity they contribute to an organization, they cannot compensate for weak or ineffective processes forever. Frequently, organizations rely on individual or team heroics to overcome fundamentally flawed processes. In the long run, your best bet for beating your competition in the marketplace is to fix the processes based on the insight of your star performers. As Rummler and Brache noted, "Processes are rolling along (or frequently stumbling along) in organizations, whether we attend to them or not. We have two choices—we can ignore processes and hope that they do what we wish, or we can understand them and manage them."[1]

> *As good as exemplary performers are at their jobs, and despite the productivity they contribute to an organization, they cannot compensate for weak or ineffective processes forever.*

One of the distinguishing characteristics of exemplary performers is that they have already optimized the existing processes in order to produce their exceptional results. When we do performance analysis on exemplars, we often find that they have made modifications to the organization's standard processes. These modifications might include:

- Eliminating tasks and steps which add little or no value;
- Adding tasks and steps that their experience has shown to be of high value; or
- Shifting the process metrics that they use in their mental model from lagging to leading indicators.

Here are two examples of how top performers shift from lagging to leading indicators. First, we have consistently seen that high-performing salespeople do not typically focus on quota attainment. They exceed quota quarter after quarter by identifying indicators that are good predictors of performance, two or three quarters into the future. These predictive activities may include:

- How many times they interact with the client organization;
- At what level these interactions occur;

- Business and market trends impacting the client organization; and
- How well they have succeeded at establishing well-positioned internal customer advocates.

In the second example, our client's highest-performing R&D team had developed predictive indicators to help estimate the probability of a commercial product evolving from a particular line of research. This allowed them to consistently make better decisions within the R&D process concerning which projects to accelerate, which to halt, and where to most effectively invest resources.

As we described earlier, high performers are often unconsciously competent and are not able to share their expertise to refine and improve critical processes without external support. And unfortunately, without direct help, organizations are not able to leverage or replicate this unconscious expertise to drive greater results.

Therefore, in order to optimally shift the performance curve, you will want to eliminate the barriers within your current processes that have been discovered and addressed by your stars. There is one caution, however: Some individuals who produce these exceptional results may violate parts of the process in ways that are unsafe, costly to others, or perhaps unethical. These individuals are *not* star performers. Star performers achieve their exceptional results while *still* adhering to corporate guidance in the area of safety, and so on.

In order to replicate the activities of your exemplary performers, you must use what you have learned from them to improve process effectiveness and efficiency. For example, organizational redesign serves no purpose if it doesn't improve process performance; thus, lessons learned from your exemplars provide invaluable input during an organizational redesign. Likewise, jobs should be designed so that individuals can contribute effectively to produce the process outputs.

Job Design

To achieve optimal job design, you need to take the same systems view we discussed at the organizational and process levels. You cannot optimize the performance of people in a vacuum. You must look at their work in the context of the other two levels and ensure that the design of the job or role integrates smoothly into the wider organizational and process design.

Unfortunately, this cross-level approach to optimizing performance is not what our practice commonly encounters. What we see most frequently within our clients' organizations are the following one-size-fits-all approaches to increasing performance:

- Train them
- Coach them
- Threaten them
- Discipline them
- Transfer them
- Replace them

Notice the recurring theme—*them!* There is an underlying assumption that all is well within the organization except for the performance of the people. This assumption is as illogical as believing that all automotive problems are due to a faulty electrical system. You must differentiate between the symptom and the root cause of the performance problem.

Rummler and Brache describe this as the "human performance system" and argue that the system needs to be as carefully and intentionally designed as the organizational system and the processes within it.[2] What follows is a more complete explanation of the major components of the human performance system to further illustrate this point:

- *Inputs*: These are the raw materials, assignments, peer and customer requests, and so forth, that call people to take action.
- *Performers*: These are the individuals or teams who convert inputs to outputs. Every role is required to produce outputs or accomplishments. If your immediate response to this is to push back and say, "At my level I am only expected to think and conceptualize. I have no responsibility to produce any tangible outputs," our response would be that if you produce no outputs you are, by definition, not producing any value. It may be difficult to clearly define those outputs in the beginning, but every role of value to the enterprise is producing significant accomplishments.

- *Outputs/Accomplishments*: Part of the organizational and cultural bias that has existed for a hundred years in North America is to focus more on the actions and activities of people versus their outputs or accomplishments. We argue strongly that it is impossible to optimize the performance of people if you focus on and measure their *activities* versus their *outputs*. Busy people are not necessarily high-performing people. High-performing people consistently produce superior results, whether or not they are exceptionally busy.
- *Consequences*: These are the positive and negative effects that performers experience when they produce an output to standard. Positive consequences could include extra compensation, recognition within or without the organization, assignments, more challenging work, and so forth. Negative consequences include disciplinary action, reassignment, and termination.
- *Feedback*: This is information concerning the individual's performance. Feedback should start with information about the quality, cost, quantity, and timeliness of the outputs. More detailed feedback concerning their activities and tasks should only be provided when and if the outputs are not meeting standards. Feedback may come in the form of oral or written comments, error reports including statistical data, customer feedback, and performance appraisals.

When we discuss the performance curve, the horizontal axis is always a measure of the quality, quantity, and timeliness of an individual's or team's accomplishments (see Figure 1.4 on page 17). In order to optimize these outputs, you need to systematically analyze and improve each of the human performance system components as part of an integrated whole.

The key performance variables within the human performance system are:

- *Job Goals*: A clear link must be established between goals for processes, functions, and roles so that individual workers are able to optimize the performance of the processes within which they work. These goals communicate to the performers what they are expected to produce, along with the key success metrics. The best way to build a clear understanding and commitment to these goals is to involve your people in the process of establishing these goals.

- *Job Design*: Every job should be structured so that it maximizes the probability that the job's goals will be achieved. We often find that jobs are not clearly designed in a way that supports the accomplishments management expects from a particular role. Jobs frequently are cluttered with ancillary responsibilities that are not necessarily aligned with the true goals. When this happens, role clarity for the job is diminished and the performers are distracted, which directly affects their ability to perform to standards.

  A key tool to provide greater job clarity is "swim lane" process mapping. This approach to process mapping allows you to clearly identify how multiple roles support the success of a process. It also makes key handoffs clear and transparent, while offering explicit opportunities to improve process flow and to provide greater clarity in support of job design.

- *Job Management*: The role of managers is to manage the five components of the performance system. In our approach to optimizing performance, the manager's role is to facilitate the production of the accomplishments for each position reporting to him or her, by ensuring capable people are operating in a barrier-free work environment.

The manager needs to provide clear performance specifications. Not only must such standards exist, but the performers must be aware of the standards and believe that they are achievable. The manager must also provide the required task support so that the performers are able to clearly recognize the inputs that require action on their part. The employees must also be able to execute the required tasks without interference from other tasks. And clearly, the resources (materials, time, tools, and information) need to be available and adequate.

In addition, managers need to provide appropriate and timely consequences to the performers. However, the consequences must support the desired performance and be accurate, timely, relevant, specific, easy to understand, and meaningful to the individual performers.

The preceding section addressing *organizational design, process design*, and *job design* will provide you with the necessary insights concerning intentional design of integrated, barrier-free work systems. Our practice indicates there is significant upside potential in systematically addressing these variables in an integrated fashion. As the next section outlines, physical or motivational conditions can also have a significant impact, either facilitating or hampering individual or team performance.

Physical Conditions

Listing all options under this category is not possible. However, the following questions can help as you assess the "barrier-free" nature of your particular work environment.

Resources

- Are the requisite resources or process inputs available in sufficient quantity to meet the needs of your team?
- Are the resources available in close proximity to the point of need?

Ergonomics

- Does the workspace provide adequate flexibility for both individual and team-based activities?
- Is there sufficient lighting to support the nature of the work? Is the area free of glare?
- Is the noise level appropriate for the nature of the work?
- Does the available seating adjust to meet the needs of the workers? Does it provide adequate support?
- Do adequate work surfaces exist at an appropriate height for the work to be performed?
- Is the work area clean, and is ventilation adequate?

Safety

- Is the workspace free of safety hazards such as slippery surfaces, low-hanging objects, fumes, and so on?
- If applicable, do all workers have access to appropriate safety equipment such as goggles, hardhats, and the like?
- Are hazardous areas and equipment clearly labeled?

Motivational Conditions

The following questions will help you assess the current work environment to discover whether motivational conditions are having unintended negative consequences:

- Are the employees in your organization provided with clear criteria for judging their own performance? Do employees have explicit standards for their results in terms of quantity, quality, and timeliness?
- Do employees understand the "worth of their work"? Do they understand how their accomplishments fit into the overall strategy and success of the organization? Do they have a clear understanding of their downstream customers and the potential impact on those customers if their outputs are inadequate in any way?
- Do employees receive timely feedback on their performance?
- Is the workload manageable? Are goals achievable? If appropriate, can employees control the pace of their work?
- Are high performers "punished" by regularly being assigned additional work on top of their completed assignments?

As noted, these questions simply represent a range of potential issues that stand in the way of high performance. As you develop your own high-performance systems, you'll identify the specific issues and questions appropriate for your own organization and the industry in which it operates.

Summary

This chapter gave you a sense of the upside potential to be found by improving the work design, the physical conditions, and the motivational conditions for job performers. These factors and their proper alignment are illustrated in Figure 12.3. When we intentionally align the six subsystems represented in the figure, we truly enable exemplary performance. This is our role as leaders—developing high-performing individuals and teams who routinely produce accomplishments that meet or exceed expectations!

Notes

1. Geary Rummler and Alan Brache, *Improving Performance: Managing the White Space on the Organizational Chart* (San Francisco: Jossey-Bass, 1995), 44.
2. Ibid., 65–66.

| Just Imagine ...

By this point we are sure you have been considering opportunities within your own organization to drive exemplary performance by applying the approaches we've recommended. Perhaps you have already identified one or more critical roles where:

- The performance is absolutely essential to implementing the company's strategic direction.
- There is wide and unacceptable variance between the majority of incumbents and your stars.

Imagine the possibilities if you act on the premise that the talent curve does not predetermine the performance curve. You have read about how to create models of optimal performance based on the insights of your stars. You know you can use the Profiles of Exemplary Performance to:

- Provide precise expectations that clarify for everyone in your organization exactly what is expected and to eliminate conflicting goals and feedback;
- Assign your employees to jobs that enable them to perform at the top of their game with the right skills and tools for producing the desired results;
- Create a work environment and culture that are conducive to outstanding performance on a day-in and day-out basis;

- Equip your team with the relevant skills, knowledge, and information they need to excel at their work; and
- Ensure that everyone in the company, from bottom to top, feels that he or she is an integral member of a successful team.

What would it look like if you, as leader and architect of your organization, designed a barrier-free, high-performing work environment and your team's performance curve shifted optimally to the right? What would be the impact if you closed the gap between average performers and star performers by 10%, 20%, or 30%? *You now have a model for shifting the performance curve for your own department, team, or organization.*

Simply put, shifting the performance curve is all about driving results, enhancing revenue, and improving margins. Our model and methodology allow organizations, their leaders, and associated work teams to capture more value with existing resources. In a "do more with less" economy, this is the right strategy for these times, clearly differentiating you from your competition. Exemplary performance is not reserved for just a few individuals—it is an achievable goal for the great majority of executives, managers, teams, and individual contributors. Your goal is to maximize value, as shown in Figure 13.1.

Figure 13.1. Maximizing Value

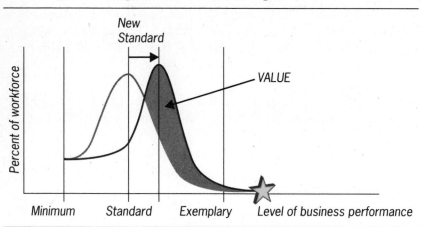

Source: Exemplary Performance, LLC.

You've read the book—now turn your knowledge into action. Take the next step!

Sample Data for One Accomplishment

Major Accomplishment: Valid, Healthy Pipeline

Time Spent: 5%–10%
Importance: Important
Difficulty: Moderate Difficulty
Major Criteria
- Percentages spread over pipeline are sufficient to deliver revenue quota each quarter.
- Opportunities in pipeline are balanced between short-term and long-term sales cycles.
- Number of opportunities is valid.
- Opportunities are qualified at correct levels, per company guidance.

Interactions
- People: Sales manager, customers, virtual team members
- Tools/resources—CRM system, personal spreadsheet

Influences
- Facilitators: Sales portal
- Barriers
  - Lack of time and discipline
  - Sales portal too "clunky/complex," drop-down menus are confusing, resulting to errors in classification
  - CRM system doesn't provide all necessary data

Task List

1. Build individual business plan.
2. Identify sales opportunities with account team.
3. Identify sales opportunities with partners.
4. Tier opportunities in order to allocate resources.
5. Conduct sales activities and marketing programs to obtain additional prospects.
6. Track opportunities in CRM system.
7. Qualify prospects using provided criteria.
8. Participate in pipeline review meetings to determine next step to advance deals.
9. Build and maintain trustworthy personal relationships with internal and external sales resources.

Task Details for Major Accomplishment — Valid, Healthy Pipeline

Task 1: Build Individual Business Plan

Stimulus/Cue: Beginning of fiscal year
Task Output: Annual individual business plan of activities
Success Criteria—plan is complete, actionable, and includes the following:

- Definition of solution focus
- Key account decision makers defined
- Marketing plan that includes specific events and campaigns
- Defines revenue level threshold to determine pursuit/no pursuit
- Identifies partners
- Includes competitive overview
- Defines engagement process
- Establishes goals to be met (revenue number, and so on)

Critical Aspects: Defining your solution focus
Speed Required: Not important
Frequency Performed: Unpredictable
Consequences/Impact Rating: High
Complexity Rating: High
Likelihood of Change in Way Task Performed: Unlikely

Influences on Performance
- Facilitators—Mandated by leadership; template of previous best practice
- Barriers—Lack of guidance on defining solution focus and selecting partners

Task 2: Identify Sales Opportunities with Account Team

Stimulus/Cue: Beginning of fiscal year/quarter
Task Output: Account plan
Success Criteria
- Mutually agreed to roles and responsibilities
- Enterprise accounts have been identified
- Identify top five strategic accounts per account manager; revenue objectives for each strategic account
- High-visibility potential opportunities identified for each account
- Time frame for execution established

Critical aspects: Setting virtual team expectations; proactively obtain commitment for regular involvement by virtual team members; understanding account manager goals and objectives for each strategic account
Speed Required: Not important
Frequency Performed: Unpredictable
Consequences/Impact Rating: Moderate
Complexity Rating: Moderate
Likelihood of Change in Way Task Performed: Unlikely
Influences on Performance
- Facilitators—Prior FY revenue results; background info on account—annual report, and so on.
- Barriers—AM unprepared or resources are unavailable

Task 3: Identify Sales Opportunities with Partners

Stimulus/Cue: Beginning of fiscal year/quarter
Task Output: Territory

Success Criteria

- Three to five key partners
- 50 accounts; adequate marketing events; clear results criteria (revenue objectives or numbers of deals)
- Revenue performance objectives are set

Critical Aspects: Setting mutual partner expectations; engage partner ASAP with an opportunity; understand partner's business to help in selection
Speed Required: Not important
Frequency Performed: Unpredictable
Consequences/Impact Rating: Moderate
Complexity Rating: Moderate
Likelihood of Change in Way Task Performed: Unlikely
Influences on Performance

- Facilitators—Partner/manager involvement in partner selection; individual business plan
- Barriers—No template available; lack of info on partner's business

Task 4: Tier Opportunities in Order to Allocate Resources

Stimulus/Cue: Receive lead (from account manager, other employees, events, partners, RFPs)
Task Output: Decision to retain or delegate opportunities based on priority
Success Criteria—decision based on:

- Revenue size and established budget
- Strategic importance
- Timeframe (will close in fiscal year)
- Probability of success
- Comprehension of customer decision-making process and knowledge of key decision maker
- Partner acceptance
- Competition analysis

Critical Aspects: Having the right intelligence; existing executive relationship
Speed Required: Not important

Frequency Performed: Weekly
Consequences/Impact Rating: Moderate
Complexity Rating: Moderate
Likelihood of Change in Way Task Performed: Unlikely
Influences on Performance

- Facilitators—Availability of valid information
- Barriers—No formal tool or process; inaccurate information; insufficient customer data

Task 5: Conduct Sales Activities and Marketing Programs to Obtain Additional Prospects

Stimulus/Cue: Individual business plan (personal)
Task Output: Additional prospects and opportunities
Success Criteria

- Five qualified opportunities per event

Critical Aspects: Making personal contact with invitees; having high-quality attendees
Speed Required: Not important
Frequency Performed: Unpredictable
Consequences/Impact Rating: Moderate
Complexity Rating: Moderate
Likelihood of Change in Way Task Performed: Likely; more targeted events based on better lists with personal follow-up
Influences on Performance

- Facilitators—HQ sales; strong local marketing liaison; experience with campaigns
- Barriers—CRM system has insufficient/inaccurate info on accounts; HQ sales bandwidth

Task 6: Track Opportunities in CRM System

Stimulus/Cue: Update of an opportunity when over 20%
Task Output: Accurate information within CRM system
Success Criteria

- Accurate data by month's end
- Should be done daily

Critical Aspects: Use of opportunity categorization drop-down menus; CRM system skills
Speed Required: Not important
Frequency Performed: Unpredictable
Consequences/Impact Rating: High
Complexity Rating: High
Likelihood of Change in Way Task Performed: Unlikely
Influences on Performance

- Facilitators—CRM system training
- Barriers—CRM system training not specific/mapped to functions to be executed; takes time from actual selling

Task 7: Qualify Prospects Using Company Sales Process Criteria (such as 10%, 40%, 60%)

Stimulus/Cue: Customer input about opportunity status
Task Output: Accurate data in pipeline for each opportunity
Success Criteria

- Timely (to support forecast)
- Matches criteria

Critical Aspects: Ask right questions to determine percentage; ensure consistency with sales process criteria; be conservative on forecasting
Speed Required: Not important
Frequency Performed: Unpredictable
Consequences/Impact Rating: High
Complexity Rating: Moderate
Likelihood of Change in Way Task Performed: Unlikely
Influences on Performance

- Facilitators—Sales process; portal
- Barriers—Lack of or ineffective customer feedback

Task 8: Participate in Pipeline Review Meetings to Determine Next Step to Advance Deals

Stimulus/Cue: Updates to opportunities based on company sales process criteria/milestones.
Task Output: Tasks and activities with identified owners

Success Criteria
- Clear list of next steps
- Ownership is clear (successful delegation and agreed to)

Critical Aspects: Ensuring clarity of actionable steps
Speed Required: Not important
Frequency Performed: Daily
Consequences/Impact Rating: High
Complexity Rating: Low
Likelihood of Change in Way Task Performed: Unlikely
Influences on Performance
- Facilitators—Personal spreadsheet; HQ sales team spreadsheet; portal for milestone validation
- Barriers—Lack of regular updates to CRM system; lack of personal discipline

Task 9: Build and Maintain Trustworthy Personal Relationships with Internal and External Sales Resources

Stimulus/Cue: In business plan; change of personnel
Task Output: Trustworthy personal relationships with internal and external sales resources (partners, marketing, HQ sales, product marketing, and so forth)
Success Criteria
- Mutual open-door relationship, mutual follow-through, reciprocity on both sides

Critical Aspects: Recognize there are many partners and don't show favoritism; being truthful and honest in all dealings; respect confidentiality
Speed Required: Not important
Frequency Performed: Weekly
Consequences/Impact Rating: Moderate
Complexity Rating: Low
Likelihood of Change in Way Task Performed: Unlikely
Influences on Performance
- Facilitators—Knowing who to call; knowing strengths of partners in your geo
- Barriers—Bandwidth; clarity of the partner/manager role

The Authors

Paul H. Elliott, PhD

Paul H. Elliott is the president and founder of Exemplary Performance, LLC (EP), based in Annapolis, Maryland. Dr. Elliott's expertise is in the analysis of human performance, the design of interventions that optimize human performance in support of business goals, and strategies for transitioning from tactical to strategic approaches. Dr. Elliott assists organizations in performance analysis, product and process launch support, design of advanced training systems, and the design and implementation of integrated performance interventions.

Prior to starting EP in 2004, Dr. Elliott was a Fellow with Saba Software of Redwood Shores, California. There he provided thought leadership in both the services and product strategy of the company. From 1995 through 2001, Dr. Elliott was president of Human Performance Technologies, LLC (HPT), a leading provider of methodologies and training for performance consultants.

From 1988 through 1995, Dr. Elliott was vice president of RWD Technologies. He consulted on approaches to improve human performance across diverse industries, which included telecommunications, financial services, automotive manufacturing, petrochemical, and consumer products. Throughout the course of Dr. Elliott's consulting career, he has worked with organizations such as Microsoft, P&G, FedEx, BellSouth, Ford Motor, Boeing, BP Exploration & Production, Agilent, Valero, and other Fortune 500 organizations.

Dr. Elliott served on the Board of Directors of the American Society for Training and Development (1993–1995). He received his PhD in educational psychology from the University of Illinois (1975), his MS from Syracuse University (1972) and his BA from Rutgers University (1970). Publications include a chapter in *The ASTD Handbook for Workplace Learning Professionals* (2008) entitled "Identifying Performance and Learning Gaps" and an article in the June 2005 issue of ASTD's journal, *T&D*, entitled "Making the Exemplary Normal." Dr. Elliott also wrote the chapter on "Assessment" in *Moving from Training to Performance*, edited by Dana Gaines Robinson and James C. Robinson (ASTD & Berrett-Koehler, May 1998) and "Job Aids" in the *Handbook of Human Performance Technology*, edited by Harold Stolovitch and Erica Keeps (ISPI & Jossey-Bass, March 1999).

Alfred C. Folsom, PhD

Dr. Folsom is the chief performance officer and vice president of Operations at Exemplary Performance, LLC, based in Annapolis, Maryland, where he brings over twenty-five years of experience in the field of Human Performance Technology (HPT). His most recent work has been helping people and organizations make the transformation to strategic work as strategic business partners and performance consultants. Other recent projects include helping incorporate lessons learned from the Deepwater Horizon Oil Spill response; in high-tech software sales; underwriters of commercial insurance; medical testing laboratories, and federal work in the area of Search and Rescue.

Dr. Folsom's expertise is in the area of HPT and its specific application throughout the United States Coast Guard, where he retired as a Captain (O-6) after twenty-four years of commissioned service. He is a 1984 graduate of the U.S. Coast Guard Academy, in New London, Connecticut, and served his last tour as chief of the Office of Training, Workforce Performance and Development at Coast Guard Headquarters. In that role, he was the program manager for Coast Guard Training, which included responsibility for six Training Centers, two Training Support Commands, and more than twenty-four thousand students annually. Additionally, he served as a board member of the ISPI Advocates and was on the steering committee for the Interservice Training Review Organization (DOD) and on various committees with the annual

Interservice and Industry Training, Simulation and Education Conference.

In addition to his bachelor's degree, Dr. Folsom holds an MBA from the Florida Institute of Technology and a PhD in instructional systems from Penn State. Following graduate school, Dr. Folsom was part of the stand-up of the Coast Guard's Performance Technology Center in Yorktown, Virginia. He was also the lead Human Performance Technologist on the Coast Guard's Joint Rating Review—which resulted in the largest workforce restructuring since WWII.

Dr. Folsom joined Exemplary Performance in April 2008 and was the recipient of the inaugural award of the ISPI Potomac Chapter for Outstanding Contributions to the field of Human Performance Technology.

Index

A

A-players: determining strategic, 23–24; helping B-players perform like, 110–111; putting in A-positions, 25; talent retention strategies for, 75

"A Players or A Positions?" (Huselid, Beatty, and Becker), 24

A-positions: determining strategic, 23–25; differentiating high/low performance in, 29–31; putting A-players in, 25; shifting performance curve for people in, 28

About this book, 17–19

Accomplishments: capturing star's, 57–59; clarifying how they support goals, 149–150; as component in human performance system, 209; defining clearly expected, 28, 119–120; determining exemplary performance's key, 64–68; determining job fit using, 190–192, 196–199; discerning whether individual or team output, 40–41; measuring activity vs., 13–14; precision of criteria required

for, 111; producing value with, 14, 66; recognition for, 136, 137–138; sample data for, 217–223; task lists for, 65–67; vs. behavior, 13. *See also* Outputs; Tasks

Agilent, 137

Aging, 159

Aligning: priorities to strategies, 22–29; project to strategy and goals, 60–62; recognition and rewards to values, 100, 126

American Taekwondo Association (ATA), 136

Americans with Disabilities Act (ADA), 198

Analysis. *See* Conducting performance analysis

Apple, 110

Armed Services Vocational Aptitude Battery (ASVAB), 186–187

Armstrong, Lance, 86

Assumptions. *See* Myths about star performers

Attention, 147

Axelrod, B., 75, 182

B

B-players, 110–111

Barriers: eliminating unintended, 198–201; impediments in